Women
AS CHRIST'S DISCIPLES

By Boyd Luter

Looking Back, Moving On: Applying Biblical Principles of Freedom to Your Life

By Boyd Luter and Kathy McReynolds

Truthful Living: What Christianity Really Teaches about Recovery

Disciplined Living: What the New Testament Teaches about Recovery and Discipleship

Women

AS CHRIST'S DISCIPLES

BOYD LUTER
AND KATHY MCREYNOLDS

Baker Books

A Division of Baker Book House Co
Grand Rapids, Michigan 49516

Published by Baker Books
a division of Baker Book House Company
P.O. Box 6287, Grand Rapids, MI 49516-6287

Printed in the United States of America

Library of Congress Cataloging-in-Publication Data
Luter, Boyd.
  Women as Christ's disciples / Boyd Luter and Kathy McReynolds.
      p.   cm.
  Includes bibliographical references.
  ISBN 0-8010-5711-6 (pbk.)
    1. Women—Religious life. 2. Women in the Bible. 3. Bible. N.T.—
Biography. 4. Christian life—Biblical teaching. I. McReynolds, Kathy,
1960– . II. Title.
BV4527.L88   1996
225.9'22'082—dc20   96-32480

CONTENTS

INTRODUCTION

It would not be a great surprise if many readers approached this book with initial questions similar to this one: Why would two traditionalist, evangelical Christians choose to write a book on the distinctive New Testament angle of discipleship for women in the mid–1990s? Before answering that question, though, it is helpful to expose some questionable assumptions that may be lying in wait for such a question.

We all have assumptions. They serve as tinted glasses through which we view questions and reason toward answers or solutions. Unfortunately, though, not all assumptions are created equal. Some are quite accurate, others are only slightly imbalanced, while still others are heavily distorted.

Let's take a good look at some assumptions we may have about New Testament discipleship and women. First, it's assumed in some evangelical circles that biblically consistent Christians simply wouldn't write a book on this subject. Why? Because this is supposed to be the questionable turf of the radical feminist fringe element.

A second common, but less-than-accurate, assumption has to do with the amount of writing on discipleship that has already been done. Frankly, in the minds of some discipleship experts and many evangelical publishing houses, virtually the final word on discipleship was said and written in the 1970s, the so-called "Decade of Discipleship."[1]

A third shortsighted assumption concludes that there isn't enough of a distinctive angle on discipleship related to women seen in the New Testament to justify such a full-length treatment. After all, it is reasoned, none of the Twelve whom Jesus trained nor the early spotlighted teachers in the church in Acts were women. In fact, isn't only one woman (Dorcas, in Acts 9:36) actually called an individual disciple?

A fourth off-the-mark assumption is often made because of the mood of the 1990s. This is a time of megachurches and user-friendly church growth. For the most part, discipleship has been reduced to a cherished verity. It is assumed by many to be basically a dinosaur—a reminder of an era gone by for evangelicals approaching middle age and certain parachurch ministries.

Probably the most foundational erroneous assumption, though, has to do with who would read a book like this and what difference they could make. Some assume that only women's ministry leaders and a few other women would be willing to get into a subject like distinctive biblical discipleship for women.

Correcting Mistaken Assumptions

Let's take another, more thoughtful, look at these five assumptions, in reverse order. As to who would read a discussion of key women disciples in the New Testament, women's ministries are, in fact, a great starting point. The roles of women's ministry leaders and directors (and, in some cases, pastors) usually exist because ministry to and by individual women is quite active and rapidly expanding.

The reality is that many evangelical churches are about 55 percent female from the young adult stage upward. Thus, pastors and other wider ministry overseers simply cannot afford to ignore what impacts the majority of the adults under their ministry umbrella.

In looking at the mood of the 1990s, we have seen plenty of evidence through our ministries and wider contacts that neither discipleship nor biblical commitments are out-of-date. Perhaps certain forms of discipleship that were trendy in the late '60s and '70s have declined in popularity. If anything, though, the publication of Mike Wilkins's ambitious work on discipleship, *Following the Master: Discipleship in the Footsteps of Jesus*,[2] in 1992 indicates that the '90s are not shaping up to be an antidiscipleship wasteland.

In regard to whether there is a sufficiently distinctive angle of discipleship for women in the New Testament, you need search no further than Luke and Acts to establish that there is. In Luke 14:26–33 Jesus states three times that a person cannot be his disciple (vv. 26, 27, 33) unless certain commitments and priorities are present in that person's life. As will be discussed elsewhere in the book, more often than not, it was certain women in the life and ministry of Jesus Christ[3] (seen primarily in Luke's Gospel) and in the early church[4] (primarily in Acts) who exemplified these ideals for discipleship.

Admittedly, the New Testament emphasis on the discipleship of women is less extensive and more subtle than that of men. But, as will be seen, it is undeniably present and significant.

Reflecting on the mountain of writing that was done on discipleship in the 1970s, two things should be clarified:

1. In spite of all the writing in that period, there was actually very little fresh biblical thinking that came about. Most of the scriptural concepts were copied from a few influential leaders of the unofficial evangelical discipleship movement.
2. Since most of the discipleship emphasis in the 1970s was parachurch, relatively little was ever developed regarding discipleship directly related to the local

church as seen in Acts and the New Testament Epistles.[5] Thus the mass of writing of the 1970s largely occurred within a fairly narrow and incomplete scope of New Testament teaching and application.

Finally, what of the thought that only hard-core feminists would write about women and discipleship? Think about it. Should only Baptists write about baptism? Should only charismatics write about spiritual gifts (Greek *charismata*)? Should only Presbyterians write about presbyters (i.e., elders in the church)?

We could go on, but the point should be clear enough: The best way to move toward a balanced biblical position on a subject—in this case, women as disciples in the New Testament—is for more believers, not just those with a narrow or single-issue focus, to carefully examine the scriptural teaching. Through close biblical study (Acts 17:11), we must make sure that what is being taught in evangelical circles represents "the truth, the whole truth, and nothing but the truth."

Looming Need, Large Challenge

Having thought through these issues and others, we firmly concluded that there was more than enough reason—even need—for a fresh look at women as disciples in the New Testament. In doing so, we also realized that there existed a sizable amount of material and fresh angles that were not even close to adequately explored.[6]

That point must be coupled with the perception of many rank-and-file American evangelicals that women were, at best, second-class disciples in the New Testament. To the extent that a counter-case has been attempted to be made, it has been largely undercut by the feminist persuasion of its advocates.[7]

We chose to work together on this book because of our friendship, similar convictions, and previous experience writing together.[8] We also brought complementary areas of expertise to the project. For example, Kathy wrote most of the entries on the key women (and one of the men) discussed in this book for the recently published *The Complete Who's Who of the Bible* reference project.[9] On the other hand, besides writing articles and a doctoral dissertation on discipleship issues, Boyd also contributed a couple of related entries to *Who's Who*[10] and did the "Great Commission" entry for the *Anchor Bible Dictionary*.[11]

The complementary nature of this project also can be seen in the somewhat different writing style in some of the chapters. Boyd sought to draw on certain breakthrough research he had done. Through coursework at Talbot School of Theology and other related writing, he discovered a number of fresh angles that will do the following:

1. serve as a meaningful personal challenge to anyone interested in New Testament women or discipleship
2. give various women disciples in the New Testament more of their just due in terms of demonstrating the important roles that they played
3. be useful in the ongoing discussions on women's ministry

Meanwhile, as Kathy did her thorough biblical preparation, she was more often gripped by the emotional and relational tensions that the female disciples faced and worked through to grow as disciples. She was thus able to consistently identify with such struggles and vividly portray them, while at the same time carefully surveying what can be known of the characters from a scriptural standpoint and background study.

The resulting overall mix is carefully blended, with each contributing both from the head and the heart. We readily acknowledge what the Lord has taught us, individually and through "iron sharpens iron" interaction (Prov. 27:17). We trust that he will use what we have found and presented "for the equipping of the saints" and "the building up of the body of Christ" (Eph. 4:12), to his glory.

We will be your guides in understanding and coming to a deeper appreciation of those wonderful models of discipleship in the New Testament who are women. May you be blessed in your walk with the Lord as you join us in the chapters ahead!

Part 1

Women Disciples during Christ's Ministry

One

Unexpected Disciples and the Great Commission

Toward the beginning of a class on the Great Commission and discipleship I was teaching several years ago, a student posed an excellent question: "Is there a special kind of discipleship related to women seen in the New Testament?"

My hesitant answer was a stumbling baby step that eventually led in the direction of the writing of this book: "I really don't know . . . though I suspect that there *is* a uniquely female angle on discipleship in the New Testament. However, to be perfectly honest, it will take some additional study and thinking for me to answer that question."

What an understatement! Over the next weeks, I alternately drilled some dry holes and struck several gushers in this pursuit of the New Testament teaching on women as Christ's disciples.

Finally, near the end of that semester, I met with the student to share what I had found. Happily, the sketchy material delighted the student. But it did not really satisfy me. If anything, I felt I had barely scratched the surface. So, I determined I'd continue my scriptural detective work in earnest.

Silence or Subtlety?

Over time, it became clear to me that the biggest factor of confusion in studying New Testament discipleship as it relates to women is that only one woman is specifically called a "disciple." That woman is Tabitha (or Dorcas) in Acts 9:36, who is described as a *mathetria*, which means "female disciple." But such terminology is not the only way that a disciple is identified in the New Testament.

This was reminiscent of a similar apparent problem involved in earlier research and writing I had done on the general concept of disciple making.[1] The specific words *mathetes* ("disciple") and *matheteuo* ("make a disciple of") are both quite common in the Gospels and Acts, but they are not found at all in the Epistles and Revelation. Because of this obvious and unexpected absence, there has been a tendency to act as if Matthew through Acts are the only books of the New Testament that have anything to say about discipleship. That is very nearsighted, since Christ commanded his followers to "make disciples" until "the end of the age" (Matt. 28:19–20). After all, the rest of the New Testament is, so to speak, the "beginning of the age." It is still necessary, however, to try to come up with some kind of explanation for this troubling absence.

It seemed that this vacuum of standard discipleship terminology after the Book of Acts had to be due to one of two reasons: Either, (1) the apostles simply ignored the priorities laid out by the risen Lord in his Great Commission, or, (2) they continued to deal with the concepts of discipleship but shifted to different wording.

Of course, the first option is almost unthinkable, and fortunately the second clearly proves to be the case. In the Book of Acts, *disciples* is found to be interchangeable with *church, saints, believers,* and other terms (e.g., Acts 11:26). These trade-off terms then show up in force in the Epistles and Revelation. Thus, the full equivalent of discipleship, as well as explanations on the carrying out of the Great Commission, is indeed present beyond Acts in the New Testament, though expressed other ways than in the Gospels.[2]

Some of these other ways to determine that people are being viewed as disciples in the New Testament when the expected terms don't appear are:

1. When *follow* (Greek *akolutheo*) speaks of following Jesus, it means going after Jesus as a disciple.
2. When the expression "with Him" (e.g., Luke 8:1–3) indicates spending time with Jesus, it means as his disciple.
3. Sitting at the feet of a recognized teacher (e.g., Luke 10:39) was the normal posture of a disciple.
4. Compare the individual's level of commitment to what Christ laid out as the cost of discipleship in Luke 14:26–33.

As will be seen in the pages ahead, each of these (and more) is applied to women in the New Testament as disciples of Christ.

Christ's Commission in Context

The best way to come to appreciate the presence of women disciples in the New Testament, however, is to study the Great Commission in context. In fact, in preparing to write this book, I was overwhelmed in that regard because I found so much more than originally anticipated. The female disciples are not only there at the most difficult and dangerous point in the biblical record of Jesus' ministry, but they play indispensable roles as models of Christ's marching orders for his church until "the end of the age" (Matt. 28:20).[3]

First, though, a quick survey of the Great Commission. Five passages in the Gospels and Acts combine to produce the overall shape of Christ's Commission: Matthew 28:19–20; Luke 24:46–49; John 20:21–23; Acts 1:8; and, traditionally, Mark 16:15–18.[4] Matthew 28 is the best known of the five and often called "the Great Commission" in its own right. However, Christ's command in Matthew meshes together in complete harmony with the other four versions.

Table 1 visualizes how these passages complement one another. Each provides its own slant on carrying out the risen Lord's Commission. Leaving any of the five out impoverishes our understanding of what Jesus Christ called his people to be about until the end of the age (Matt. 28:20), to the ends of the earth (Acts 1:8).

Yet, even with an understanding of all the vital parts of the Great Commission, it's still way too easy to miss the important role of the women disciples. Certainly, the presence of women in the various passages that lead up to the various Commission statements is obvious (Matt. 27:56, 61; 28:1–8; Mark 15:40–41, 47; 16:1–8; Luke 23:49, 55; 24:1–10; John 19:25–27; 20:1, 11–18; Acts 1:14). But it is frequently overlooked just how closely these contexts tie the women to those statements.

This reveals a foundational point for our entire study of New Testament women who are disciples of Christ: *When Jesus gives his apostles the commands to make disciples and witness, the closest contextual examples of being a disciple and a witness are the women disciples.* So it is vitally important to carefully consider the presence and roles of the women seen in each of the Great Commission contexts. Each passage provides a striking artistic portrait of women disciples that goes hand-in-hand with the others.

Go and Make Disciples

The risen Savior's strategy was simple yet profound when he explained what he meant by "make disciples of all the

Table 1
The Great Commission

Feature	Matt. 28:19–20	Luke 24:46–49	Acts 1:8	John 20:21–23	Mark 16:15–18
Basis of Commission	"All authority" (v. 18)	Fulfillment of O.T. in death/resurrection	Resurrection appearances	Resurrection appearances	Resurrection appearances
Main Thrust	"Make disciples" (v. 19)	Proclaim repentance (v. 47)	"Be My witnesses"	Sending (v. 21)	"Preach the gospel" (v. 15)
Scope	"All the nations" (v. 19)	"All the nations" (v. 47)	Jerusalem . . . to the ends of the earth	"Any" (v. 23) (See John 3:16)	"All the world . . . all creation" (v. 15)
Procedure	Going (v. 19) Baptizing (v. 19) Teaching (v. 20)	"Beginning from Jerusalem" (v. 47)	Move out from Jerusalem (implied)	Forgive or retain sins (v. 23)	Preach (v. 15) Baptize (v. 16)
Function	Disciplemakers (v. 19)	Heralds (v. 47), witnesses (v. 48)	Witnesses	Sent ones (v. 21) Forgivers (v. 23)	Heralds (v. 15)
Empowering	"I am with you . . . to the end of the age" (v. 20)	"Power from on high" (v. 49)	Holy Spirit comes upon you	Holy Spirit (v. 22)	"In My name" (v. 17)
Duration/Extent	Implied: End of age/all nations (vv. 19–20)	All nations (implied, v. 47)	Ends of the earth	Any (implied, v. 23)	World, creation (implied, v. 15)

nations" (Matt. 28:19). The structure of the passage[5] indicates that the heart of disciple making is as simple to understand as "1, 2, 3":

1. *Going* in evangelism (v. 19a)
2. *Baptizing* the converts (v. 19b)
3. *Teaching* the baptized disciples to grow through obedience to the Lord's standards (v. 20a)

Sadly, those who have studied and written on disciple making have often run roughshod over both the structure of Matthew 28:19–20 and the immediate context. The general consensus is that "make disciples" must mean trying to duplicate the same process Jesus used with the twelve apostles, as seen in much of the Lord's public ministry in Matthew. After all, weren't the remaining eleven disciples the ones who originally heard Christ give his Commission (see Matt. 28:16)? And, wouldn't they naturally reflect on their own experience in being trained by the *perfect* discipler?

Such reasoning, however, does not take into account four realities that are easily seen in Matthew:

1. When Jesus was arrested in the Garden of Gethsemane, those handpicked eleven disciples all "left Him and fled" (Matt. 26:56), seriously calling into question the quality of their discipleship.
2. It is the *women* who are spotlighted as disciples as they continue to follow (Matt. 27:55; Greek *akolutheo*)[6] Christ to the cross and tomb, along with Joseph of Arimathea, who had "become a disciple" (Matt. 27:57; Greek *matheteuo,* the same word translated "make disciples" in 28:19).
3. The women at the empty tomb were the first disciples to witness the resurrection of Christ and the ones instructed to inform the apostles (Matt. 28:5–10).

4. Since there is absolutely no other mention of Jesus or his disciples baptizing earlier in Matthew,[7] in commanding "baptizing" (28:19) Jesus could not have been inferring in his Commission that they make disciples exactly the way he did in his previous ministry with the Twelve (which included Judas). For when this presumed "training of the Twelve" approach was really put to the test, the reactions were betrayal, fleeing, and denial—hardly the stuff of exemplary discipleship.

When these factors are considered, two far-reaching conclusions emerge: First, the process of disciple making laid out in Matthew 28:19–20 seems to be tailored to the setting after the resurrection in which the Great Commission must be carried out. Second, since the Commission does not read "make apostles" (i.e., focusing on how the Twelve were trained for their unique roles), our recognized models of the nature and process of discipleship should certainly include those disciples whose commitment is seen to be more consistent than the apostles. In the context immediately preceding Christ's climactic command in Matthew 27–28 (and in the other Gospels, as will be seen), that would mean the women disciples.

Related points are made by observing the beautiful inverted structure (i.e., second half paralleling ideas in the first half)[8] of this wider passage that bridges from the death of Christ on the cross (Matt. 27:50) all the way to the Commission (28:16–20), which emphasizes the role of the women disciples (see table 2). For example, it is amazing to note that the women are mentioned four times—more often than any other character except Jesus.

When this literary structure is considered holistically, it becomes clear that the women were the only disciples present at both the crucifixion (Matt. 27:55–56) and burial

(27:61) of Jesus, and they were the first ones to see him resurrected (28:9–10). They were, in effect, commissioned by
the risen Lord to take word of his resurrection to the Eleven
(28:10), which adds enormous dignity to their apparent role
at the climax of the Gospel of Matthew.

Table 2
Inverted Structure of Matthew 27:50–28:20

    A. (27:50–53) Crucified Jesus dies, causing many effects, includ-
ing the resurrecting of many Jewish saints[9]

       B. (27:54) Centurion speaks the truth about the crucified
Christ

         C. (27:55–56) *Women disciples* who followed and served[10]
Jesus viewing the cross (with a painful silence about
the Eleven)

           D. (27:57–60) Joseph of Arimathea, a disciple who
courageously buried Jesus in his personal tomb

              E. (27:61) *Women disciples* followed Jesus' body
to the tomb in the evening (see 27:57)

                 F. (27:62–66) Jewish leaders attempt to
secure the tomb against the resurrection
of Christ

              E'. (28:1) *Women disciples* return to the tomb at
early dawn on the Sabbath

           D'. (28:2–4) Guards terrified by the angel at the
tomb

         C'. (28:5–10) *Women disciples* see the risen Christ and are
sent to inform the Eleven (see 28:16)

       B'. (28:11–15) Guards bribed to lie about the empty tomb

    A'. (28:16–20) Resurrected Jesus commissions making disciples
of all the nations until "the end of the age"[11]

What was that role? There seems good reason to conclude that Matthew is presenting the women as the consistent, courageous model disciples who bridge from the
cross to the concluding Commission in the troubling absence of the eleven apostles.

Fearful, but Present, Disciples

When we turn our attention to the Gospel of Mark, there are more similarities than differences with what has been found in Matthew. However, the differences are important in understanding the role of the women disciples of Jesus Christ. Those differences include one very significant addition (to what Matthew included), two purposeful deletions, and another long-debated possible deletion or change.

The addition has to do with Mark's description of the women disciples viewing the crucifixion. After naming the same three women (Mark 15:40) as in Matthew 27:56[12] the passage refers to "many other women who had come up with Him to Jerusalem" (Mark 15:41). Though not specifically numbered, there definitely were other women followers (i.e., disciples) of Jesus beyond those clearly named in the Gospel passages.

The first deletion has to do with any mention of the Jewish leaders or Roman guards, both of which played prominent roles in Matthew (27:62–66; 28:2–4, 11–15). In their absence, the narrative starting at Mark 15:40 describes only those who are disciples of Jesus (although the fact that Joseph of Arimathea[13] is a disciple, clearly stated in Matt. 27:57, has to be inferred from Mark 15:43–46). The majority of attention is paid to the female disciples (15:40–41; 15:47–16:9)—a truly remarkable proportion for a heavily patriarchal period of history.

The second deletion, which is more subtle, has to do with the mention of fear (Mark 16:8; see Matt. 28:8) without the "great joy" (Matt. 28:8) that had energized the women disciples in Matthew. If the shorter ending of Mark at 16:8 (the long-debated deletion) is correct, the women disciples' fearful silence is the troubling parting word of the second Gospel.

Even if the longer concluding section (Mark 16:9–20) is accepted, as in the King James and New King James versions, the women's fear fits in with the pattern of fear and unbelief that is part of Mark's unsettling portrait of discipleship. When it is remembered, however, that the eleven remaining apostles all fled in the Garden of Gethsemane (Mark 14:50) and didn't listen to Mary Magdalene (16:9–11), having to be rebuked by Christ for "unbelief and hardness of heart" (16:14), we realize that the portrait of women disciples in Mark is no put-down.

It is also the case that the narrative in Mark 15–16 has at least as elaborate a parallel structure as that seen in Matthew 27–28. The women disciples are again mentioned four times around references to other characters. As seen in table 3, they become the dominant characters in view as you move into the resurrection account presented by Mark.

If this structure is on target, the message of Jesus' resurrection is, as in Matthew, climactically entrusted to the fearful women disciples (Mark 16:7–8). What a heavy responsibility! But what better role and at what better time could Jesus have chosen to underline the tremendous significance of the women?

Witnesses Who Are Ignored

Doubly amazing, there is not just one inverted structure in the vicinity of the Great Commission in Luke but two. Consistent with what has been seen in Matthew and Mark, both emphasize the role of women as disciples of Jesus Christ.

This double chiasm (another term for inverted structure) has a wider double focus, but the twin spotlights are complementary: the crucifixion, death, and burial of Jesus in Luke 23:26–53, and then the response to the resurrection and empty tomb in Luke 23:54–24:49.

Table 3

Inverted Structure of Mark 15:12–16:8

A. (15:12–15) Pilate fails to release Jesus and has him flogged and crucified

  B. (15:16–20) Jesus mockingly paid homage as King of the Jews in the Praetorium

    C. (15:21) Simon of Cyrene forced to carry the cross

      D. (15:22–23) The place of crucifixion, where Jesus declines spiced drink

        E. (15:24) Jesus crucified and clothes divided

          F. (15:25–27) Jesus crucified as criminal but called king

            G. (15:29–30) Crowds insult the crucified Jesus

              H. (15:31–32) Jewish leaders and criminals mockingly call Jesus "the King of Israel"

                I. (15:33) Darkness over the earth

                  J. (15:34) Jesus cries out that he's been forsaken by God (cf. Ps. 22:1)

                    K. (15:35) Mistake about Elijah

                      L. (15:36a) Jesus offered the drink of a common laborer-servant[14]

                    K'. (15:36b) Mistake about Elijah

                  J'. (15:37) Jesus cries out and dies

                I'. (15:38) Veil of temple torn in two

              H'. (15:39) Roman centurion calls Jesus "the Son of God"

            G'. (15:40–41) Group of *women disciples* view Jesus' crucifixion

          F'. (15:42–45) Jesus buried in rich man's tomb

        E'. (15:46a) Jesus' body wrapped in linen and buried

      D'. (15:46b–16:1) The place of burial, where *women* came to put spices on Jesus' body

    C'. (16:2–3) *Women* voluntarily go to Jesus' tomb

  B'. (16:4–6) Jesus' resurrection proclaimed by an angel at the tomb

A'. (16:7–8) *Women* fail to go tell the disciples and Peter about the resurrection

By contrast with Matthew and Mark, mention of the women disciples is found just once in the first structure (Luke 23:49), though in a highly significant way. In the second structure, a lengthy view of the women is seen in Luke 23:55–24:12, then a central remembering of their witness is found in Luke 24:22–24.

Thus, though these female disciples play an important role among the many witnesses to Jesus' death in Luke's first chiasm, it is considerably stronger in the second. Aside from the risen Lord, they're the only positive characters focused on in that part of the narrative of the resurrection. Tables 4 and 5 reflect the key roles of the women disciples in these passages.

Unless the inverted structure of the crucifixion and burial passage is properly appreciated, it appears that the women in Luke 23:49 are mentioned merely as part of the larger crowd watching Jesus suffer on the cross. Even noting that *accompanied* is a translation of the Greek word *sunakoloutheo,* which very likely speaks of discipleship,[15] does not capture the full significance of their role in this context.

However, as seen in table 4 in the mirroring structure of Luke 23:26–53, the women disciples are paired with the women of Jerusalem, who also followed (Greek *akoloutheo*) Jesus out to Calvary. Those women were weeping for Jesus but would have more reason to weep for themselves in the time ahead (23:27–31).[16] On the other hand, the women disciples would grieve only until they were the first to find out about Jesus' resurrection (24:1–10).

Even though the women disciples are only specifically mentioned once in this structure, that inclusion is doubly significant because of who is *not* included. Though other friends from Galilee were present, none of the apostles were anywhere to be found (23:49). Again, to the extent that the disciples of Jesus were represented at all at the cross, these women were those representative disciples.

Nor did the women disciples turn away or distance themselves even after Jesus died. They courageously followed

Table 4

Inverted Structure of Luke 23:26–53

A. (23:26) Someone else (Simon of Cyrene) carries Jesus' cross

  B. (23:27–31) Crowd and *women* of Jerusalem, following Jesus

    C. (23:32–38) Jesus crucified and heckled as crowd watches spectacle

      D. (23:39–43) The criminal's witness to Jesus' innocence

        E. (23:44–46) Someone else (the Father) causes apocalyptic effects and receives Jesus' spirit at death

      D'. (23:47) The centurion's witness to Jesus' righteousness

    C'. (23:48) Jesus' crucifixion watched as a spectacle by a crowd

  B'. (23:49) Acquaintances and *women* who followed Jesus from Galilee

A'. (23:50–53) Someone else (Joseph of Arimathea) provides Jesus' tomb

Joseph of Arimathea to the tomb (23:55). Then, as soon as reverence for the Sabbath permitted, they returned to the tomb (23:56–24:1).

They didn't expect what they found: an empty grave (24:2–3)! Next, two angels appear, who tell them of the resurrection and remind them Jesus had predicted it (24:4–7). According to Luke (consistent with Matthew and Mark), that means the women were the only disciples present at the first appearance of the resurrected Jesus. It also meant that they were the logical ones to immediately go and inform the eleven remaining apostles about what had happened (24:8–9). Luke makes clear that a number of other trustworthy female disciples (see Luke 8:1–3) went to give their testimony to the apostles and "all the rest" (24:9).

Sadly, neither the apostles (24:11) nor the other disciples (24:22–25) would believe them. Table 5 shows how Luke cleverly underlines the women disciples' role in stark contrast to the unbelief of the other disciples.

Table 5
Inverted Structure of Luke 23:54–24:49
  A. (23:54–24:12) *Women disciples* witnessing Jesus' empty tomb
     are not believed when they witness to the apostles (except
     possibly Peter)
     B. (24:13–21) Jesus not recognized by two disciples on the
        Emmaus Road
        C. (24:22–24) Amazing witness of the *women disciples* to
           the empty tomb of Jesus restated
     B′. (24:25–35) Jesus recognized by the two disciples through
         explanation of Scripture and the breaking of the bread
  A′. (24:36–49) Jesus recognized by his physical presence with the
      apostles and gives the Great Commission to witness to all
      nations (through God-given power)

The three Synoptic Gospels (Matthew, Mark, and Luke)
each focus to a truly surprising degree on the presence of
women disciples at the crucifixion and empty tomb of Jesus.
The impression is definitely left that they, not the apostles,
are the Gospel writers' candidates for disciples to be emulated in a crisis. They were present at Jesus' lowest point at
the cross, and they were honored to be the first witnesses
to his resurrection.

Beyond Seeing to Believing

Unlike Matthew, Mark, and Luke, no clever literary
structure has been detected in the Gospel of John that calls
attention to women disciples. That doesn't mean, however,
that women are not present or that they are deemphasized.
  Again, women are clearly in evidence at the foot of the
cross in John 19:25–27. Again, a woman disciple (Mary
Magdalene) is the first follower of Jesus to arrive at the
empty tomb (John 20:1). John sees fit to give an even longer
version of Mary meeting angels and then Jesus himself at
the tomb (20:11–17). In John, Mary Magdalene is the car-
rier of the news of both the empty tomb (20:2) and the resurrected Lord (20:18) to other disciples.

If there is a literary touch in this section of John's Gospel that spotlights a woman disciple, it's a bookend effect created by the repeated wording, "for fear of the Jews," in 19:38 and 20:19. That wording is found elsewhere in John only in 7:13, where it speaks of why many Jews would not openly seek Jesus. This observation makes the courage of Mary Magdalene stand out all the more.

"Fear of the Jews" indicates why Joseph of Arimathea hadn't come forward as a disciple earlier (John 19:38) as well as why the apostles were cowering behind closed doors (20:19). By contrast, first Mary Magdalene boldly went to the tomb of Jesus "while it was still dark" (20:1), then Simon Peter and the "beloved disciple"[17] went as it was becoming broad daylight (20:2–8). Mary Magdalene is a wonderful example of courageous trust for disciples of all time.

In terms of the Great Commission, it's no coincidence that the risen Lord Jesus sends Mary Magdalene to his "brethren" (20:17) just before the apostles receive Christ's command, sending them out with the message of forgiveness in the power of the Holy Spirit (20:21–23). So Mary became the Gospel of John's first messenger commissioned by the risen Christ.

Partners in Prayer for Pentecost

Our last cameo scene of women disciples in close proximity to the Great Commission is found in Acts 1, where certain female disciples are part of the prayer meeting preparing for the day of Pentecost in Acts 2.[18] There's no elaborate structure here, as in the Synoptic Gospels, but Luke dignifies the role of the women in this foundational season of prayer in the upper room (Acts 1:13–14). This passage talks about their oneness and the persistence of their prayers. What's amazing, though, is that the women and Jesus' half brothers are placed on equal footing with Peter, John, and the other apostles in this scene.[19]

After Peter's incredible sermon in Acts 2, the infant church is seen "continually devoting themselves" to foundational spiritual growth activities, including prayer (2:42). They're also described as "continuing with one mind" (2:46). Thus in the freshly received New Covenant power of the Holy Spirit, much of the agenda for the people of God echoes Acts 1:14, "These all with one mind were continually devoting themselves to prayer."

Interestingly the apostles felt the urgent necessity of returning to this pattern in Acts 6:4: "We will devote ourselves to prayer." They had become distracted with trying to take care of all the needy people (4:32–37; 6:1) and reuniting the church in Jerusalem after the tragic Ananias and Sapphira episode (5:1–11), which had caused them to lapse temporarily from their priorities of prayer and God's Word (6:2–4).

The bottom line here is that the pattern for the church seen in Acts 2:42–47 (add also Paul's "pray without ceasing" command in 1 Thess. 5:17) started in the upper room before Pentecost. In that regard, Acts 1:13–14 can only be treated fairly if it's remembered that women disciples were a key part of that unity in prayer.

You Can Be My Disciple If . . .

In this initial quest to locate women disciples in the New Testament, we must not overlook Luke 14:26–33. There Jesus clearly lays out the "radical commitment"[20] he asks of those who follow him in discipleship (and disciple making; Matt. 28:19–20). If this lifestyle is not pursued, Jesus tersely says, you "cannot be My disciple" (Luke 14:26, 27, 33).

The flip side of that statement is crucial here. It means that, if a person *does* display that kind of "radical commitment," he or she *is* a disciple. When a careful search of the New Testament is made for those who have counted the cost, the result is a sizable number of women who make the grade as disciples. (That is especially evident when we also consider the other clues that identify disciples that were mentioned earlier in this chapter.)

In the Gospel of Luke alone we have many examples of women who qualify as disciples:

Elizabeth, the mother of John the Baptist (Luke 1)
Mary, the mother of Jesus (Luke 1, 2, 24)
Anna, the prophetess (Luke 2:36–38)
Mary Magdalene (Luke 8:1–3; 23:49–24:10)
Joanna and Susanna (Luke 8:1–3)
Mary and Martha of Bethany (Luke 10:38–42)

There are also a sizable number of other women disciples in Luke whose specific names are not given (Luke 8:1–3; 23:49–24:10). In the Gospel of John, even the Samaritan woman (John 4:1–42) and the woman caught in adultery (John 8:1–11)[21] are in the fold.

Venturing into Acts, Dorcas is actually stated to be a disciple (Acts 9:36); Lydia certainly proved to be (Acts 16:14–15, 40); and there can be no question about Priscilla (Acts 18:1–3, 24–28). In the Epistles, a number of women in Romans 16 stand out as disciples by virtue of Paul's descriptions, and Timothy's mother, Eunice (2 Tim. 1:5), emerges as a wonderful model for discipleship.

As will be seen in the following chapters, each woman disciple is an absolutely fascinating person in her own right. Also, it will become abundantly clear that each struggled with personal circumstances in carving out her commitment as a disciple. While they are unquestionably first and foremost disciples of the Lord Jesus, their discipleship will be seen to include uniquely feminine touches.

Two

MARY

Mother, Fellow Sufferer, Faithful Disciple

If you were given a multiple-choice test with the following question, how would you answer?

Who was Mary of Nazareth?
    (a) the mother of Jesus
    (b) a fellow sufferer
    (c) a faithful disciple

Chances are pretty good that you would choose answer *a*. To identify the virgin Mary as a fellow sufferer or a faithful disciple would probably be the farthest thing from your mind.

Mary's unique role as the mother of Jesus has made her a household name and has given her a prominent place in world history. As significant as this role is, however, it is not all that can be said about Mary. In this chapter we will become more intimately acquainted with her as the mother of Jesus, but more important, we will come to know her as a fellow sufferer and faithful disciple.

Before we explore the New Testament Scriptures concerning Mary, we must briefly discuss the two main contemporary views about her. One is the traditional Catholic view, which upholds her as the Mother of God, one who is sinless and one to whom we can pray.[1] The other view, which is basically the more Protestant one, simply sees her as an ordinary young woman, whose quiet demeanor and naivete reflected her time and culture.

These two somewhat extreme views, while unbalanced and unbiblical in some respects, do represent the life of Mary to some degree. She was indeed "the mother of our Lord" (Luke 1:43) and a woman whose gentle behavior was highly esteemed in her day,[2] but these two views are essentially incomplete. The New Testament portrayal of Mary, which is complete with colorful glimpses of her unique role and reverent personality, is nothing less than fascinating.

Her journey from being the young mother of the Son of God to being a faithful disciple of the Son of God was a rough one at times, which makes her life all the more intriguing. From the angel's greeting to her in Luke 1:28 to the little prayer meeting she attended in the upper room in Acts 1:13–14, Mary has much to teach us about women as Christ's disciples. The place to start our journey is at the very beginning: a look at Mary's family history.

The Right Pedigree

In order to understand a little about what Mary was made of, it is important to consider her family background. The genealogies in Matthew 1 and Luke 3 provide us with some necessary information. We know from several Old Testament passages that the Messiah was to descend from the tribe of Judah and, more specifically, was to be of the lineage of King David. Matthew traces the Messiah's genealogy through Abraham while Luke goes back even further to Adam.

Because of the Old Testament prophecies, it was necessary to show that Jesus was born to parents (Joseph, his stepfather, and especially Mary, his birth mother) who were of the right stock. Therefore, the significance of the genealogical records in Matthew and Luke cannot be understated. It is generally agreed that Matthew contains Joseph's genealogy and Luke traces Mary's.[3] If this view is correct, Joseph's genealogy probably shows Christ's royal and legal right to the throne of David, while Mary's genealogy, since it goes all the way back to Adam, possibly emphasizes Christ's connection to the entire human race. The point is that both genealogies support the fact that Joseph and Mary were qualified, legally and relationally, to be the parents of the Messiah.

As a descendant of David, Mary had a rich heritage. She had royal blood flowing through her veins. This was no small thing. She was well aware that someday the Messiah himself, the Savior of Israel, would come through a member of her own family line. But little did she know just how intimately involved she would be in the Messiah's coming. Her lineage made her a rightful candidate to bear God's Son, but it was her godly character that ultimately qualified her to be his mother.

An Unexpected Pregnancy

Prior to writing this book, I was surprised by an unexpected pregnancy. It took me a while to get over the shock, especially since I had just had my first child seven months earlier. I remember getting on my knees at that time and praying that God would give me the heart of Mary in this situation. Like her, I wanted to be able to say, "I am the Lord's servant. . . . May it be to me as you have said" (Luke 1:38 NIV). Not long after that prayer I felt a peace in my heart that God was in control.

Needless to say, my own surprise and shock over an unplanned pregnancy certainly cannot be compared with what Mary must have experienced when she learned that she would have a baby. After all, when the angel Gabriel came to her in Nazareth and announced the good news, she was pledged to be married to Joseph, but she was still a virgin (Luke 1:26–27)! Could there be some kind of mistake?

Even though Gabriel's words troubled Mary, there was no mistake. She was the right young woman, one who was "highly favored" by the Lord (Luke 1:28 NIV). Liefeld states that the Greek word *(kecharitomene)* rendered "highly favored" is significant because it actually means she is a recipient of God's grace.[4] She who would bear the One "full of grace and truth" (John 1:14) was herself a recipient of God's grace.

Mary had found favor (grace) with God, and that favor would be poured out on all people through the divine offspring she would bear. Her child would actually be God's own Son. He would reign on David's throne forever and receive a kingdom that would never end (Luke 1:30–33).

We all know the Christmas story quite well, but think about it from Mary's perspective for a moment. Here she is, a virgin. Not only is she told that she will soon become pregnant, but the child she will bear will be the long-awaited Messiah himself—the fulfillment of all God's promises to Israel. What unbelievable news. What is truly amazing, however, is that Mary believes it. Her question "How can this be?" (Luke 1:34) is not an indication of doubt but simply an inquiry of how this will be accomplished, since she is a virgin.

When Mary is informed by Gabriel that her child would be supernaturally conceived by the Holy Spirit (vv. 35–37), she reverently responds by saying, "I am the Lord's servant. . . . May it be to me as you have said" (v. 38). What a statement of faith! Luke brings her incredible faith into sharper focus by contrasting it with Zechariah's apparent doubt (Luke 1:18–20). Tucker and Liefeld offer further insight into Luke's purpose in contrasting the two:

> Two contrasting figures appear at the opening of the Christian era: an old man and a young girl. In separate narratives, Luke's literary artistry draws attention first to one and then to the other.
>
> He is Zechariah, resident of Jerusalem, the centuries-old religious center of Judaism. A priest whose knowledge of divine things has been seasoned with years. . . .
>
> She is Mary, resident of Nazareth, a small village removed both in distance and in spirit from Jerusalem. A young teenager whose knowledge of God has been fostered by deep insight into the Scriptures. . . .
>
> Zechariah doubted, but Mary believed. Perhaps the symbolism is unintentional on Luke's part, but it is there nevertheless: the old era, long past with the close of the Old Testament, receives its final reprise with the incredulity of a man. The new era, about to be proclaimed in the gospel of Jesus Christ, begins with the faith of a woman.[5]

So significant is Mary's faith that Luke would devote his considerable literary talents to emphasizing it. Not only does her reverent faith stand out, but her humility and submission to God's will serve as an example to all female (and male) disciples today. Yes, she is Mary, the mother of our Lord (Luke 1:43), but she is also Mary, an ordinary woman with extraordinary faith and outstanding character.

Mary went to share her incredible life-giving message with Elizabeth, who herself had already enjoyed a sort of life from death experience: the opening of her barren womb.

Mary went to encourage her relative and share in her joy. But, as it turned out, it was really Mary who was encouraged and overjoyed by their encounter.

Sharing the Incredible Truth

Gabriel informed Mary that her relative, Elizabeth,[6] was also expecting a child and was in her sixth month. Mary quickly left her home in Nazareth and headed for the Judean countryside (about fifty to seventy miles from Nazareth) to see Elizabeth (Luke 1:39–40). Mary didn't even have to verbally share the good news. As soon as she greeted Elizabeth, the baby in Elizabeth's womb (John the Baptist) leaped for joy (v. 41).

Elizabeth was then filled with the Holy Spirit and blessed Mary and the Child she was to bear. God had actually been very gracious to both Mary and Elizabeth. Hence, they both equally had a lot to share about their unexpected experiences.[7] There is no question that they both had experienced a miracle.

The focus of the passage, however, is not on both of them but on Mary. Luke uses this occasion to call attention to Mary's faith (v. 45). Consequently he clues us in on the significance of this scene. Elizabeth, through the power of the Holy Spirit, validates Mary's faith, praising her for believing all that God said to her. This must have been a tremendous encouragement to Mary. God had previously spoken to her through the angel Gabriel, but now she is hearing about his purposes through her own relative, Elizabeth.

As it turns out, Mary, who went to share the incredible truth with Elizabeth, was herself strengthened by hearing the truth from her. Luke, under the inspiration of the Holy Spirit, calls attention to Mary's exemplary faith and demonstrates how God encourages the faith of a faithful disciple (2 Chron. 16:9). Mary was so excited by Elizabeth's blessing that a song of joy welled up in her heart.

A Song in Her Heart

Mary's inspired song (Luke 1:46–55), known as the Magnificat,[8] is a remarkable testimony to Mary's knowledge of many Old Testament themes, especially salvation. It brilliantly shows her insight into God's plan and purposes for his people. The Old Testament phraseology and concepts she uses are reminiscent of Hannah's song in 1 Samuel 2:1–10.

Many scholars believe that Hannah's song served as a model for Mary,[9] but her similarity with this great Old Testament saint goes far beyond composing poems. Mary's godly character and attitude of servanthood echo back to Hannah. Mary possibly thought of Hannah, who put herself at the Lord's disposal and gave up her son, Samuel (1 Sam. 1:28), when she submitted herself to God to carry his Son.

The biblical truth weaved throughout Mary's song can teach us much about the character of God and his purposes in salvation history (Luke 1:50–51), but it also teaches us something about Mary that is highly relevant to our topic of women as Christ's disciples. Her song reveals that she was a learner of God before she became a disciple of Christ. She was a follower of God in the way of the Old Covenant.

There can be no doubt that Mary was a learned woman. Even in this way she serves as an excellent model for us to grow in the knowledge of God and to keep growing. As we shall see, she continued to grow and learn, especially when it came to being the mother and disciple of Jesus. It is at this point that we begin to see Mary in a different light, when we get to know her as a fellow sufferer and faithful disciple.

The New Way—in a Manger

Because we are all different, the path to discipleship will take us in some unique directions. But Mary's path was unique in the truest sense of the word. For one thing, she had to learn a new way of relating to her God, the Initiator of the Old Covenant, the God she had known and served all of her life. Also, her path to discipleship started with an angel's announcement of a supernatural pregnancy. This is truly a unique beginning!

Mary's pregnancy ended in an ordinary manner except that the birthplace was highly peculiar: a stable (Luke 2:7). It was probably the last place she ever thought she'd be for such a monumental event. Think about it—the Son of God born among straw and animal dung? Already Mary was learning something new about her God: He sometimes does things in a most unorthodox manner. Her relationship with him was to continue to surprise her, ever growing and deepening with his every cry and her every motherly response.

God was doing a new thing among his people, and Mary was the first to witness it. She had always expected God to act on behalf of his people, but this was beyond her wildest dreams. As we noted in the previous section, Mary was a faithful follower of God and well acquainted with his promises of redemption. As her song revealed, she was confident that God would come through; he would send the Messiah.

Mary had this hope in her heart and, like other faithful Jews, anticipated the day when he would come. But that she would be chosen to play such a significant role in the blessed event, Mary could not have imagined. She would be the one to deliver the Deliverer? She would be the one to bear the Bearer of the New Covenant? Yes, she was the one. And the Way of salvation now lay before her in a manger.

To be sure, Mary was going to face some unique challenges. She was going to have to learn from her Babe how to relate to God in the new way. She would raise him, but he would ultimately raise her up to be a disciple.

Needless to say, being Jesus' mother added a unique and sometimes complicated dimension to the discipleship process.

For instance, her motherly instinct would naturally produce in her certain attitudes and actions, but that motherly instinct would not give her an advantage in the discipleship process or make the transition into discipleship any easier. Discipleship is not a natural and easy process for anyone, but that was especially true for Mary, who knew Jesus first as her son.

The things she would naturally do as his mother she would have to learn to do as his disciple. As his mother she would naturally love him, but as his disciple she would have to learn to love him as her Savior and Lord. As his mother she would naturally provide for him, but as his disciple she would have to learn to trust in his providence. As his mother she would naturally sacrifice for him, but as his disciple she would have to learn from him the deeper meaning of a sacrificial life.

Did Mary ever ponder any of this as she beheld her precious little son lying in the manger? Did she ever think at all about the challenges that lay ahead of her? Maybe. When the shepherds came to them in Bethlehem and told of all the Lord had spoken to them concerning the child (Luke 2:8–18), Luke says that Mary "treasured up all these things, pondering them in her heart" (v. 19).

Matthew did not record Mary's reaction when the Magi came and bowed down to worship her newborn son (Matt. 2:11), but it is safe to assume that she continued to ponder these things in her heart. The shepherds' words and the Magi's actions probably overwhelmed her. It's possible that she even wondered what all this meant for her in the days to come. Two recorded visits to the temple do shed some light on her future, and both visits turned out to be a lesson in discipleship for Mary.

Lessons at the Temple

Mary's first visit to the temple after Jesus' birth took place on the eighth day—the time to circumcise him. Joseph and

Mary brought Jesus to the temple to present him to the Lord and offer the prescribed sacrifices (Luke 2:21–24). Soon after they arrived, they were approached by a devout old man named Simeon (vv. 25–32). Filled with the Holy Spirit, he prophesied over the baby Jesus and spoke of his future. Jesus' parents were amazed at what Simeon said (v. 33). Then Simeon turned and spoke directly to Mary, "This child is destined to cause the falling and rising of many in Israel, and to be a sign that will be spoken against, so that the thoughts of many hearts will be revealed. *And a sword will pierce your own soul too*" (Luke 2:34–35 NIV, italics added).

As his mother, Mary would have naturally been disturbed by this prophetic word concerning her son's destiny. As his disciple, the word would have been equally disturbing. The most intimate thoughts of her heart would be revealed and laid bare before her son. She learned that his life and mission would fill her future with intense pain and suffering, both as a mother and as a disciple. This was Mary's double-edged sword.

The next temple lesson came twelve years later.[10] Joseph, Mary, and Jesus, along with many other relatives, went up to Jerusalem to celebrate the Passover (Luke 2:41–42). When the time of feasting was over, they left for Nazareth, thinking that Jesus was with them. They began to look for him in their company, and when they could not find him, they went back to Jerusalem. After three days, Joseph and Mary finally found Jesus in the temple (vv. 43–46).

Joseph and Mary were clearly anxious and upset over the situation. Mary said to him, "Son, why have you treated us like this? Your father and I have been anxiously searching for you" (v. 48 NIV). Jesus' response, "Didn't you know I had to be in my Father's house" (v. 49 NIV), and Luke's notation that they didn't understand what he was saying to them reflect Mary's (and Joseph's) continuing need to grow as a disciple (v. 50). Tucker and Liefeld say of this event:

Her question betrays both mother's natural anxiety and a lack of understanding. Jesus' reply in the following verse— "Didn't you know I had to be in my Father's house?" (or, "about my Father's business")—implies that she should have gained a sense of his special filial relationship to God the Father. This is the first clue we have that, in spite of the remarkable insights she showed in the *Magnificat*, Mary needed time to absorb the implications of her Son's person and mission. . . . Mary had to learn to follow him as a *disciple*, rather than processing and directing him as his *mother*.[11]

Luke tells us again that Mary "treasured all these things in her heart" (Luke 2:51). In other words, she considered everything that took place and was willing to learn and grow from the experience. We modern-day disciples can learn from Mary the value of willingness, of asking questions, and of searching for answers. It is comforting to know that, even as Jesus' mother, Mary did not fully understand him and had a constant need to know him better.

Mary's Growing Pains

It becomes even more clear during Jesus' earthly ministry that Mary is a fellow sufferer and faithful disciple. Her growing pains are manifested in both her words and actions, as she struggles through the transition from mother to disciple. We are given only a few glimpses of her during Christ's ministry, but what we see is quite revealing.

John's Gospel mentions Mary only two times, and in both contexts he refers to her as "the mother of Jesus" (John 2:1; 19:26–27). This is significant because in both passages she is seen with his other disciples. (John's Gospel gives no nativity story.) John portrays Mary as one who, like the others, is following Jesus.

What is also noteworthy is that in both situations Jesus is conversing with Mary, and his authority is clearly seen. Hence, these two scenes are crucial in understanding Mary as a disciple. She, like the other disciples, was there at the outset of Jesus' earthly ministry (John 2:1–11),[12] and she was also there at his death and resurrection (John 19:26–27; Luke 24:1–10). Therefore, Mary, like the other disciples, was a reliable witness to these extraordinary events.

The Wedding at Cana

It's interesting to wonder if the miracle Jesus performed at Cana, the changing of water into wine, would have ever taken place if Mary had not prompted him. It turned out to be a very serious event. John says that this miracle was his first sign, and thus his disciples (which would include Mary) put their faith in him (John 2:11).

It's important to understand that the apostle is not casting Mary in a negative light because she made this request to Jesus. To the contrary, he shows how Jesus used this interaction with his mother to show forth his glory. Tenney comments on the significance of this scene in terms of their relationship: "[Mary] acknowledged that he should act independently, and she confidently told the servants to follow his orders. She fully expected that he would take appropriate action. He did indicate that he was no longer under her authority but that he was living by a new pattern timed by the purpose of God. Jesus had begun his miracles, not at the request of earthly parents whom he still respected, but according to the purpose of his heavenly Father."[13]

The experience at Cana for Jesus was a sign of his glory, but for Mary it was a sign of her growth. She was beginning to release her son from under her authority so that she could grow in faith as his disciple. She was in essence learning to let go and grow. But this process was not always so easy for her.

Who Is My Mother?

There were times when Mary stumbled back into her old patterns of relating with Jesus. One such occasion is recorded for us in the Synoptic Gospels (Matt. 12:46–50; Mark 3:31–35; Luke 8:19–21). The Book of Mark gives us the most vivid description of this event.

During the height of his ministry, Jesus entered a certain house and a crowd gathered around him. There were so many people that he and his disciples couldn't even eat (Mark 3:20). When his family heard about this, Mark says that "they went to take charge of him, for they said, 'He is out of his mind'" (v. 21 NIV).

When Mary and his brothers arrived at the house, they immediately sent for him (vv. 31–32). Jesus' response to their request to see him probably surprised them. He looked at those gathered around him and said, "Who are my mother and brothers? . . . Here are my mother and brothers! Whoever does God's will is my brother and sister and mother" (vv. 33–35 NIV). Thus Jesus makes spiritual relationships preeminent.

This experience must have taught Mary a lot about her place in Jesus' life and ministry. The order of things was now reversed. She must become his disciple in order to become his mother. The spiritual comes first. As his natural mother, she had come to defend her son against the slander of the Pharisees, who accused him of being possessed by Beelzebub (Mark 3:22). Instead she got a lesson on the nature of spiritual relationships and learned of her need to become a member of his eternal family.

Mary's heart was in the right place. Her son was being blasphemed, and she wanted to protect him. She genuinely feared for him. A. T. Robertson says of this scene that "Mary had made a misstep, not a fatal one, but a real one, as every mother feels that she does a thousand times with her children. We can picture Mary going back to Nazareth

with her sons, but her heart was with Jesus whom she had
left behind without even a glimpse of him to see if aught
was true that she had feared."[14]

This incident clearly shows that Mary had some struggles on the road to discipleship. Her feelings toward Jesus
as his mother sometimes interfered with the discipleship
process. But she quickly learned from her mistakes. To leave
without seeing Jesus was a huge step of faith for Mary and
a marvelous indication of her growth as a disciple.

To the Cross and Beyond

The suffering and discipleship of Mary is never more
plainly seen than at the foot of Christ's cross. What a painful
experience this must have been for her—a sword piercing
her soul as Simeon had prophesied (Luke 2:35). As Jesus'
mother, Mary, had loved him, provided for him, and sac-
rificed for him. But now she stood before him as his disciple, learning about supreme love and sacrifice.

At the foot of the cross Mary had put herself entirely
under his authority. Jesus then placed her into the care of
his beloved disciple, John (John 19:26–27), not as his
mother but as his disciple. Mary stayed with John and min-
gled with the other disciples. After the ascension of Jesus,
she was with them in the upper room, praying and waiting
for the Holy Spirit (Acts 1:14).

When the time arrived, Mary was filled with the Holy
Spirit, just like the other disciples. And like the other disciples, she was empowered and sent to testify concerning
the resurrection. She had become a full-fledged disciple, but
not a perfect one. As we have seen, she had her share of
struggles. She had many unique challenges to overcome.
She had to learn from her mistakes and grow in her faith
like everyone else. Nevertheless she stands as a paragon of
virtue and a remarkable example to disciples (both male and
female) in every age.

The Value of Studying the Life of Mary

We have journeyed with Mary from the manger to the upper room. We have become more intimately acquainted with her as the mother of Jesus and have come to know her as a fellow sufferer. Most of all, we have seen her struggle and grow as a faithful disciple. She has taught us the value of obedience, of humility, of asking questions, and of seeking out answers. She has taught us that ordinary women can make extraordinary contributions to God's Kingdom.

In the entire scope of the New Testament, Mary is mentioned relatively few times. But her role as the mother of Jesus has made her one of the most popular and well-known figures of all time. Yet most of the New Testament passages reveal her as a faithful and devout learner—an aspect of her life that is not at all well known. We meet her as a youthful Old Covenant believer (Luke 1:26–55), and we leave her as a veteran disciple of Christ, praying and waiting for the Holy Spirit in the upper room (Acts 1:14).

It can be safely said, therefore, that one of the greatest values of studying the life of Mary is wrapped up in the area of discipleship. Her significant role as the devout mother of Jesus and as a faithful witness to the things he did all point to discipleship. Her life speaks volumes about the costs and rewards of discipleship.

We close with an insightful quote from Mary J. Evans that sheds further light on the New Testament Scriptures that deal with Mary and discusses the significant ways she stands as a model of discipleship for the church in every age:

> These passages bring to our attention three things about the significance of Mary. Firstly . . . Mary is a particularly significant witness of certain events in the life of Christ. Secondly, she is to be acknowledged as being blessed by God (Luke 1:42–58), and in her willing response and dedication of herself to the will of God, in her faith and in her

obedience, she is an example to be honored and imitated, as indeed are all "those who through faith and patience inherit the promises" (Hebrews 6:12). . . . Thirdly the tremendous responsibility with which Mary was entrusted, the way in which her faith, her love and her growing understanding are described, and her stance alongside the rest as they awaited the coming of the promised Holy Spirit should perhaps be seen as indications of the new status which the coming of Mary's son brought to women. . . .

She was certainly a "blessed woman" and the example of her life and in particular of her willing acceptance of and obedience to the will of God is one that any Christian can be proud to follow.[15]

Three

ELIZABETH AND ANNA

Disciples with Graying Hair

A common faulty impression about discipleship is that it's only for the young and energetic. When you run into that misunderstanding, it is usually based on two short-sighted viewpoints:

1. a selective study of disciples in the New Testament focusing almost exclusively on the relatively young apostles whom Jesus called to be with him in the Gospels
2. the high proportion of younger people involved in the various groups and programs that fueled the expanding discipleship movement in the 1970s

Both of these viewpoints, however, prove to have been acquired with blinders on. Neither takes into account the increasing complexity of almost everyone's life with the passage of time. Also, neither deals with the fact that as deeply committed younger disciples get older they often, like wine, get better.

You don't have to look far in the New Testament to see that this "discipleship is only for the young" theory just doesn't wash. Mary, the mother of Jesus, is surely middle-aged (and almost certainly widowed)[1] by the time she's said to be a follower of Jesus, standing at the foot of the cross (Matt. 27:55–56; Mark 15:41; Luke 23:49). Further, Dorcas, who's called a "disciple" in Acts 9:36, was almost certainly middle-aged (and possibly a widow also) by the time the story line of Acts focuses on her ministry, death, and resurrection in Joppa (9:36–43).[2]

There are others, also. Even in a passage normally thought to be dominated by Mary, Jesus' mother (Luke 1–2), there are two women who prove to be very significant disciples: Elizabeth, the mother of John the Baptist, and Anna, the prophetess. They had to face two of the most heartrending absences that afflict the lives of middle-aged and older women disciples. Elizabeth was childless and beyond menopause (Luke 1:7); Anna was a widow and had been for about sixty years (Luke 2:36).

Batting Leadoff for Luke

Even if you are not a baseball fan, you may be aware of the importance of who bats leadoff. It's crucial to get a good start, to get things moving, to set the pace for what comes afterward. That is equally true in a story line. The way the first characters in a plot are introduced and then developed has a great deal to do with whether the readers decide to see the story through to the end.

The writers of the Gospels understood that principle. The Gospel of Matthew starts strong with its spotlight on Joseph and Mary (Matt. 1–2). The second Gospel, Mark, moves rapidly from John the Baptist, to Jesus, to the calling of the first apostles (Mark 1:1–20). The fourth Gospel, John, begins with John the Baptist (John 1:6–28), then shifts the focus to Jesus (1:29–51).

The Gospel of Luke does not prove to be the exception to the rule. Luke has more riding on it than Matthew, Mark, or John. It's the leadoff for the Book of Acts as well. Dr. Luke not only needs to generate reader interest that will carry through to the cross and resurrection of Jesus at the end of his Gospel (Luke 23–24), he must also set things in motion for what will become the biblical history of the spread of the gospel and the Christian church to the ends of the earth in the Book of Acts.

Luke gives two of the leadoff positions to Elizabeth and Anna. Elizabeth's role is key as the mother of John the Baptist (Luke 1:57–63). Anna's role is more of a cameo, but she is still a substantial part of the supporting cast surrounding the birth and early life of Jesus Christ, the Messiah (2:36–38).

The roles of Elizabeth and Anna also preview the Book of Acts in two quite direct ways. As will be seen, the same spiritual power that energized the infant church from the day of Pentecost forward in Acts was already present in the earliest chapters of Luke's Gospel.

To be specific, as the multitude at Pentecost and as Peter speaking before the rulers and leaders of Jerusalem were "filled with the Holy Spirit" (Acts 2:4; 4:8), so were these figures of the opening chapters of Luke filled with the Holy Spirit. Along with the extraordinary statement that John the Baptist would "be filled with the Holy Spirit, while yet in his mother's womb" (Luke 1:15),[3] both of his parents, Elizabeth and Zechariah, are in the same chapter described as "filled with the Holy Spirit" (1:41, 67).[4]

In addition, after Anna met Joseph, Mary, and the baby Jesus in the temple she "spoke about the child to all who were looking forward to the redemption of Jerusalem" (Luke 2:38, NIV). In Acts, Peter and the other apostles, who had encountered the resurrected Savior (Acts 1:3–9), preached to "God-fearing Jews from every nation under heaven" (2:5 NIV) who were in Jerusalem for the feast of Pentecost (2:1).

Certainly there is much more of significance about the women disciples in Luke's leadoff narrative than has generally been recognized.

Taking Away the Anguish of Childlessness

Right after the historical prologue (Luke 1:1–4), the first part of the story Luke narrates focuses on the parents of John the Baptist. As was described in chapter 1, the device of inverted structure is used to make the point. Let your eyes move slowly through the structural diagram of that section, Luke 1:5–25 (see table 6). It demonstrates how Zechariah and Elizabeth are emphasized by mirroring ideas.

In case you haven't noticed, this is a very similar type of structure[5] to the one near the end of the Gospel of Luke (23:26–53), which was discussed in chapter 1.[6] As was the case there, the woman disciple involved here (Elizabeth) is not the main focus of the passage. However, the structure still clearly emphasizes her key role.

Also, as in Luke 23, the female disciple under consideration is not involved in dialogue with other characters. There's simply the recording of her character, her childlessness, and her gracious, unexpected pregnancy (1:5–7, 24) in keeping with the angel's promise (1:13). Thus it is the structuring of the passage by Luke that portrays the characters in living color, not just black and white.

As seen in table 6, Elizabeth's role is largely found in the bookend parts of the passage (Luke 1:5–7, 24–25), though that hardly makes her an outsider. Within such an inverted structure, the outer (A and B) layers are very often closely related to what is found at the heart of the passage. In this case, that's the astounding prediction that John the Baptist will be filled with the Holy Spirit even before his birth (1:15).

Table 6

Inverted Structure of Luke 1:5–25

   A. (1:5–6) Introducing Zechariah and Elizabeth, two righteous, blameless people
      B. (1:7) Elizabeth's childlessness, beyond childbearing age
         C. (1:8) Zechariah serving priestly duties at the temple
            D. (1:9) Zechariah chosen by lot to enter the temple and burn incense
               E. (1:10) The worshipers outside at the time of the offering
                  F. (1:11–12) Angel appears; Zechariah gripped by fear
                     G. (1:13) News: Elizabeth will bear a son, John
                        H. (1:14) Child: A joy to you and to many
                           I. (1:15a) Great in the sight of the Lord, a Nazirite
                              J. (1:15b) Filled with the Holy Spirit before birth
                           I'. (1:16) Turn many back to the Lord their God
                        H'. (1:17) Grownup: In spirit of Elijah, prepare many for the Lord
                     G' (1:18) Questioning: Old man and overage wife
                  F'. (1:19–20) Angel identifies self; Zechariah mute because of unbelief
               E'. (1:21) The worshipers waiting and wondering about the delay
            D'. (1:22) Zechariah exits the temple, recognized as mute
         C'. (1:23) Zechariah completes priestly service and returns home
      B'. (1:24) Elizabeth's pregnancy and careful seclusion
   A'. (1:25) The Lord's favor shown by taking away Elizabeth's disgrace

Zechariah[7] and Elizabeth are introduced to the readers as righteous and blameless people who haven't been able to have children and were now beyond that time of life (Luke 1:5–7). They were the kind of people who were deserving of God's favor, which is given at the end of the passage: Elizabeth becomes pregnant and overcomes her cultural disgrace (1:25). Since verse 7 had told us that Elizabeth is well past her childbearing years, her pregnancy is a real miracle recorded in understated terms (1:24).

These two unassuming people and their unlikely circumstances become the channel through which the advance man for the Messiah is born (1:13–17). Also, this situation is clearly reminiscent of the delayed birth of Isaac to Abraham and Sarah (Gen. 17, 21), the founding father and mother of Israel. That birth, though certainly not on the order of the virgin birth of Jesus Christ, was also miraculous because of the ages of both husband and wife. Another striking similarity is that just as the Lord's revelation to Abraham of the birth of Isaac caused Abraham to laugh and apparently question (Gen. 17:17), so Zechariah wondered out loud how the birth of John could possibly happen, given his age and that of his wife (Luke 1:18).

Although Elizabeth has no dialogue in this section until the end when she expresses thanks to God for taking away her disgrace (1:25), she is still vitally involved. In spite of her postmenopause stage of life, Elizabeth would become pregnant and bear John the Baptist, the one who would come in the spirit and power of Elijah to call Israel back to the Lord (Luke 1:16–17; Mal. 4:5–6). That blessed event could not happen without her.

Like Son, Like Mother

The old saying goes, "Like father, like son." In connection with the birth of John the Baptist, that gets doubly turned around. As seen in table 7, the similarity here is between mother and yet unborn son: Elizabeth and John the Baptist. Also, the son is handled first, then the mother. So, in effect, Elizabeth proves to be like John in regard to the filling of the Holy Spirit. In other words, John shares his predicted prebirth Spirit-filled status with his mother.

Table 7
Inverted Structure of Luke 1:39–45

 A. (1:39–40) Mary believes the angel, goes to Elizabeth's home, and greets her
  B. (1:41a) Upon hearing the greeting, the baby leaps in Elizabeth's womb
   C. (1:41b–42a) Elizabeth filled with the Holy Spirit and speaks
   C'. (1:42b–43) Mary and unborn child blessed, and Elizabeth favored by the presence of her Lord's mother-to-be
  B'. (1:44) Elizabeth tells that baby leaped for joy on hearing greeting
 A'. (1:45) Elizabeth blesses Mary for believing the Lord's promise

The effect of this structure on an astute reader is almost poetic. Mary had gone to visit her relative, Elizabeth,[8] immediately after the angel told Mary about Elizabeth's virtually impossible conception (1:36–37). Her trip to the home of Zechariah had been made in faith in the Lord's promise (1:31–35).

Mary's greeting when she sees Elizabeth causes the unborn John to leap for joy inside Elizabeth and Elizabeth to cry out (1:41–44). The perfectly timed movement of the baby is almost surely an indication of the filling of the Spirit "while yet in his mother's womb" (1:15). The other evidence is that the baby leaped for *joy* (1:44)—an emotion that is beyond the capability of an unborn baby. Some might say that Elizabeth was engaging in overstatement or was trusting a gut-level impression when she claimed that the baby leaped for joy at Mary's greeting. Remember, though, her words were in the power of the Holy Spirit (1:41), and joy is certainly a prominent fruit of the Holy Spirit in a person's life (Gal. 5:22). Presumably that could include an unborn person,[9] especially when that unborn person has already been prophesied to be filled with the Spirit before birth (Luke 1:15).

Normally when the relationship between generations in families is spoken of it is passing something down from parent to child, older to younger. In this case, though, something is passed *up* from an unborn baby to the parent, a reversal of the typical pattern. John, still in his mother's womb, is filled with the Spirit (1:15) and leaps for joy (1:41). Then Elizabeth also comes under the control of the Spirit and speaks to bless Mary, who was pregnant with Jesus, the Messiah (1:41–43).

Elizabeth's Spirit-guided words have, unfortunately, usually played second fiddle to Mary's longer response, often called the Magnificat. Yet it's clear that Elizabeth's blessing is the setup for Mary's response. It is even held by some that Elizabeth helped Mary compose the words of the Magnificat, since Mary stayed with Elizabeth for some three months (1:56).[10] Whatever the time sequence, though, Mary's words appear to be a further passing on of the Spirit from Elizabeth to Mary.[11]

The significance of Elizabeth's double blessing of Mary and the unborn Jesus (1:42) and professing her own awed blessedness (1:43) is vast, both for the original event and in its relevance for women disciples today. As far as Mary was concerned, it appears that Elizabeth was the first person who really understood (in the Spirit's power) what had happened in Mary's unique pregnancy by the Holy Spirit. In fact Elizabeth's support and encouragement of Mary may have been all she had at a time when even Joseph, her husband-to-be, had absolutely no clue as to what had happened (Matt. 1:18–19).

From Elizabeth's standpoint, she had been in seclusion from the time she realized she was pregnant until Mary's interaction with the angel brought about her hasty trip to Elizabeth's home (Luke 1:24–26, 39–40). Mary's visit would have also greatly encouraged Elizabeth, as well as clarified the importance of her role in God's overall plan.

At first glance, Elizabeth's and Mary's circumstances might seem to be quite different. Mary was very young; Elizabeth was well past childbearing years. Mary was not yet married; Elizabeth had been married many years. In both cases, however, their common commitment to the Lord, reflecting true discipleship even at this early point (Luke 14:26–33), prompted them to see things through to their conclusions. The way that both are described scripturally indicates that they are godly models of faith and perseverance for modern disciples.

Sadly, if both were alive today, Mary would undoubtedly be counseled to consider having an abortion just as soon as her pregnancy became known. Modern medicine would consider Elizabeth's situation every bit as much a problem pregnancy that should be terminated because of her age in having her first child. Female disciples today should carefully weigh the examples of both in making their decisions in regard to pregnancies. Certainly health and personal reputations play a part. But both God's will in bringing about the pregnancy and the significance and life potential of the child, as well as the inestimable value of life itself, must not be minimized in the overall equation.

For other disciples, female and male alike, please take it to heart that first-time mothers over forty need to be greatly encouraged. For all the joy they may feel, it is difficult carrying a baby for the first time at that age, even if they are quite healthy. If a woman has other older children, a late, surprise pregnancy can be a tremendous challenge, even to a woman of strong faith.

A Disciple Who Stood Her Ground

Because Zechariah was literally speechless, Elizabeth had to assume the role of spokesperson for the family. The structure seen below in Luke 1:57–67 shows just how crucial her tenacity proved to be in regard to the birth and naming of John the Baptist.

Table 8
Inverted Structure of Luke 1:57–67

    A. (1:57) Elizabeth gives birth after an unexpected, divinely enabled pregnancy

        B. (1:58a) Neighbors and relatives hear of God's mercy to Elizabeth

            C. (1:58b) Neighbors and relatives rejoice at the baby's birth

                D. (1:59) Neighbors and relatives want to name the baby Zechariah, after his father[12]

                    E. (1:60–61) Elizabeth insists on naming him John, even though the neighbors and relatives protest that it's not a family name

                    E′. (1:62–63a) Zechariah also writes that the baby is to be named John

                D′. (1:63b) Neighbors and relatives astonished at the baby's name

            C′. (1:64) Zechariah begins to speak again and he praises God

        B′. (1:65–66) All in the surrounding area hear of the events, wondering in fear at what the Lord would do with the child

    A′. (1:67) Zechariah unexpectedly begins to prophecy in the power of the Holy Spirit

It is obvious that Elizabeth is the focal character in the first half of the passage, while Zechariah is the spotlighted figure in the second half. Thus Elizabeth, as the family spokesperson, ends up being supported by Zechariah. This is not role reversal; it is a temporary role requirement. Elizabeth was not trying to take the role of her husband. Rather, as a committed disciple, she knew she had to stand up for what the Lord had prophesied must take place (1:13) because her mute husband couldn't.

There is another kind of reversal in the second half of the structure. Elizabeth had been filled with the Spirit and had spoken in Luke 1:42–45. Now Zechariah becomes Spirit-filled and prophecies in 1:67–79.

At least one vivid impression that Luke seeks to leave is that this is a Spirit-led family. John was filled with the Spirit from before birth (1:15), and both Elizabeth and Zechariah followed suit (1:41, 67).

Through this entire narrative, Elizabeth lives up to her godly reputation that Luke describes at the beginning. Though Zechariah had been struck mute because he doubted what the angel had told him about Elizabeth's miraculous pregnancy (1:18–20), Elizabeth is still seen to be "righteous in the sight of God, walking blamelessly in all the commandments and requirements of the Lord" (1:6).

She is undoubtedly stretched spiritually by the events of becoming John the Baptist's mother and interacting with Mary. But despite her age, she never wavers from her firm resolve to accomplish exactly what the Lord directs (1:13, 60). That is a remarkable example.

Elizabeth as a Disciple before Discipleship

How does Elizabeth's discipleship stand up at the end of the twentieth century? Very well, if the balance of her actions is allowed to speak for itself instead of being critiqued by either the assumptions of the ironclad traditionalist position or the radical feminist viewpoint.

From the beginning, Elizabeth complemented her husband very well. It was not so much that their family backgrounds were similar, though they were (Luke 1:5). Rather, it was that they were spiritually well matched and both mature before the Lord. In fact, even though the description in Luke 1:6 is cast in a very Jewish mold as far as the expressions that are used, the description of the couple is as close to the commitments of discipleship as was possible before Jesus clearly stated those standards (e.g., Luke 14:26–33).[13]

In that light, it may not be merely coincidence that the word *walking* (1:6; literally "going"; Greek *poreuomai*) is the same word that begins Matthew's version of the Great Commission (Matt. 28:19) and "all the commandments" (Luke 1:6) is also the wording for the scope of obedience to the teaching step in Matthew 28:20. It almost appears that the lifestyle of Elizabeth and Zechariah anticipates the pattern laid out by the Great Commission.

Further, the actions that both took, with the exception of Zechariah's doubting fear (Luke 1:12, 18), reflect the filling of the Spirit (1:41, 67), which must control each partner in a marriage relationship (Eph. 5:18–33). Since the Holy Spirit is clearly the dynamic of the Great Commission (Luke 24:46–49; Acts 1:8), Elizabeth and Zechariah, senior citizens though they were, serve as a first look in regard to discipleship as presented by Luke.

A Matched Pair of Prophets

Now our story shifts ahead several months. After Jesus was born to Mary in Bethlehem and was circumcised (Luke 2:1–21), he was taken to Jerusalem "to present Him to the Lord" (2:22) and offer the appropriate sacrifice in the temple (2:24). There Joseph and Mary meet two older figures who seem to further the Gospel of Luke's early emphasis on commitment befitting discipleship and the power of the

Holy Spirit. The first mentioned is a man (Simeon) and the second is a woman (Anna).[14] Though more space is given to Simeon, mostly by recording his prophecy (Luke 2:28–32, 34–35), the description of Anna's godly life (2:36–37) is as detailed as that of Simeon's (2:25–26). It should also be noticed that Simeon's meeting with the baby Messiah is the crowning event of his life before dying (2:26). On the other hand, Anna's encounter is a new beginning: She "continued to speak of Him to all those who were looking for the redemption of Jerusalem" (2:38).

Whatever surface differences existed between them, there is more that indicates that Luke is presenting Simeon and Anna as a matched pair:

1. They are both elderly, since Simeon faces impending death (2:26, 29) and Anna is eighty-four (2:37).
2. Simeon's hope in "the consolation of Israel" (2:25)[15] and "the Lord's Christ" (2:26) seems to be very close to Anna speaking of Jesus, emphasizing "the redemption of Jerusalem" (2:38).[16]
3. Both act as prophets. Anna is called a "prophetess" in 2:36, while Simeon actually prophesies in the power of the Holy Spirit, as can be inferred from 2:25–27.
4. Both are godly, committed Jewish believers. Simeon was "righteous and devout" (2:25), and Anna was described as "serving night and day with fasting and prayers" (2:37).

These striking comparisons point in the same direction as the description of Zechariah and Elizabeth in Luke 1:6. Once again it appears that Luke is highlighting a couple who were disciples before Jesus even taught on discipleship. In other words, if Simeon or Anna had still been alive thirty years later, they might well have been the kind of disciples who would have followed Jesus, even to the cross (Luke 23:49).

A Widow Indeed

There is an interesting resemblance between the description of Anna in Luke 2:36–38 and 1 Timothy 5:3–16, which lays out what the early church meant by a "widow indeed." The New International Version includes the expanded paraphrase "widows who are really in need" (5:3), apparently drawing on the clarifying description in verse 5. George Knight summarizes, "A widow really in need is all alone, has no family who cares for her, and trusts in God."[17] Significantly, 1 Timothy 5:5 states that such trust and hope is expressed in "entreaties and prayers night and day," a practice for which Anna was very well known (Luke 2:37).

Thus, though absolutely nothing is known about Anna's family or means of support, the rest of the package is remarkably close to 1 Timothy 5. Anna was "above reproach" (5:7), over sixty years old (5:9), the wife of only one man (5:9), and "having a reputation for good works" (5:10). Because of the lack of mention of other family members, nothing is known about whether she had children (or how she might have brought them up; 5:10). Also, since nothing is said about a home,[18] there is no way to find out about the hospitality factor (5:10).

In the chapter on Dorcas, I conclude that the needs of widows without support who were in the church in Jerusalem (Acts 6:1–6) and of Dorcas in Joppa (Acts 9:36–43) were almost surely a large part of the momentum toward developing a consistent approach, such as the one laid out in 1 Timothy 5. However, neither Acts 6 nor Acts 9 lays down any qualifications for those women who should be supported by the churches, those called by Paul "widows indeed." The description of godly Anna in Luke

2:36–37 seems closer to a qualifying profile than any other passage in the New Testament. Though the issue of duties for those found to be widows indeed by the standards of 1 Timothy 5:3–16 is not in view, it seems reasonable that because of their age and lack of means, prayer was a primary part of the job description (5:5). If that's correct, Anna would have been a classic model for their daily supplications (Luke 2:37). Her example would also make it clear that it is entirely possible to be an older widow but still an active, effective disciple who is fully committed to the Lord.

A Worshipful Lifestyle

Some female disciples today grew up in homes where the family went to church whenever the door was open out of a sense of compulsion. Such consistent "churchianity" breeds contempt in children at least as often as it does true commitment. In fact, according to Jesus' definition of true worship as taking place "in spirit and truth" (John 4:23–24),[19] any halfhearted attendance is, at best, half-baked worship.

It takes an extraordinary person with extraordinary commitment to be involved in worship constantly without getting to where one either simply goes through the motions or runs down one's worship batteries, so to speak. Anna was definitely that extraordinary kind of person, as we will see.

Nowadays it's getting very rare to see anyone who stays with a job for an entire forty-to-fifty-year career, showing up five days a week, with only a few weeks of vacation and several assorted holidays as breaks in their same old workday world. How would it be for someone to stick with an all-day, everyday activity with no vacations for some sixty years?

That appears to have been the case with Anna. If she began her ministry of fasting and prayer shortly after her husband's death, the duration would have been about sixty years (Luke 2:36–37).

Think about it. If Anna had married in her later teens, as was common in that society, and was widowed after seven years, that would place the point of bereavement in her midtwenties. Since she was eighty-four when she had the opportunity to see the baby Jesus in the temple in Luke 2:38, it is likely that she had been a fixture in the temple precincts for well over half a century.

It is not just her length of service, though, that is so impressive about Anna the disciple—it is her bubbly enthusiasm. Rather than being cynical, or at least highly cautious, about the newest candidate for Messiah, Anna begins to thank God immediately, then continues to overflow in testimony about the newborn Redeemer (2:38), likely for the rest of her life. Admittedly, the Holy Spirit is not mentioned in the cameo appearance of Anna, but her close proximity to Simeon, who is clearly under the Spirit's control (2:25–27), implies that her spiritual secret was the "faithfulness" (Gal. 5:22) that the Spirit produces in the believer's life.

Annas in the Church Today

Too often the role of older widows in our contemporary churches is restricted to a seniors Bible study, a quilting circle, or the like. Many female disciples in their seventies and eighties are still very energetic, though. Even if they can't teach, consistently open their homes in hospitality, or do many of the other activities that characterized their earlier Christian lives, however, they can pray and thank God for what he is doing.

As Anna's life shows, a prayer warrior is not a second-class disciple. Going before the Lord in prayer and thanksgiving is as much God's will for a Christian's life (1 Thess. 5:17–18) as any other activity.

As a result of her prayer, Anna was in the right place at the right time for the phenomenal opportunity to be near the baby Jesus (Luke 2:38). Disciples today can be like Anna: They can always know that Jesus is their sympathetic high priest who is constantly available (Heb. 4:15–16). The sanctuary where he is in heaven is even better than the earthly temple where Anna served (Heb. 6:19; 8:2; 9:23–24).

Four

MARY MAGDALENE

From Slave to Servant

Never shall I forget that night, seven times cursed and
seven times sealed. Never shall I forget that smoke.
Never shall I forget the little faces of the children,
whose bodies I saw turned into wreaths of smoke
beneath a silent blue sky. Never shall I forget that noc-
turnal silence which deprived me, for all eternity, of the
desire to live. Never shall I forget those moments which
murdered my God and my soul and turned my dreams
to dust. Never shall I forget these things, even if I am
condemned to live as long as God Himself. Never.

Elie Wiesel

These are the words of a man who witnessed the horror
of a Nazi concentration camp during World War II. Elie
Wiesel wrote this some twenty years after his dreadful experience, but it reveals that the event was still a vital part of

his existence. How could he forget such misery, such suffering, such cruelty? He could not. He was hopelessly held captive by his memories.

Wiesel was forced to witness the diabolical side of humanity. This abominable experience proved to be too much for him. The images of powerful Nazi oppressors crushing and mutilating their helpless victims continually passed through his mind. He was literally enslaved to his thoughts. That unforgettable night robbed him of his desire to live.

At this point, you may be wondering: What in the world does Elie Wiesel's experience have to do with the life of Mary Magdalene? Although Mary Magdalene did not live through the horrors of the Holocaust, she did experience a season of night that could have produced in her many of the same feelings Wiesel described. Her night was one of the darkest and blackest known to the human experience. She was demon possessed and literally enslaved to evil. This was no doubt an unforgettable experience for her. It is possible that she, like Wiesel, was frequently haunted by her memories and robbed of her desire to live.

Wiesel knew firsthand the evil powers of the Nazi regime. Mary was intimately acquainted with the evil powers of the Prince of Darkness himself. Both of them were faithful witnesses of the things they saw. However, Mary's witness was quite different from Wiesel's. His was a testimony of darkness; hers was a proclamation of light. She had literally seen her God murdered and was also the first to see him risen from the dead (John 20:18). Maybe if Wiesel would have accepted her witness, he would not have been so hopelessly enslaved by the memories of his Holocaust experience.

Mary Magdalene's witness goes far beyond her verbal proclamation. When she was set free from her darkness, she became a servant to the Light (Luke 8:1–3). She moved from slave to servant. She is a remarkable example of a faithful and loyal disciple.

Not many of us have witnessed anything as horrible as the Holocaust or experienced demon possession. However, we probably have let a hurtful experience from the past block us from fully serving Christ. Mary Magdalene teaches us that our past, no matter how dark it was, need not hinder us on the path to discipleship.

We may never be able to forget our past, but we can, like Mary Magdalene, overcome it and serve Christ. Let us now examine her life and witness.[1]

Mary's Demonized Background

Mary was from a little village called Magdala[2] located on the northwest shore of the sea of Galilee. Thus "Magdalene" was probably not Mary's family name but represented her hometown. Magdala was predominately Gentile and not very well respected among the Jews. In fact, the rabbis attributed its fall to immorality.[3]

How Mary Magdalene became demon possessed is not known, but the fact that the populace of her village was largely Gentile may give some clue. Greco-Roman society as a whole was highly superstitious. Belief in magic was widespread, even among the Jews. Arnold gives us some insight into this mind-set:

> One of the clearest windows for seeing what ordinary people believed about supernatural powers in the New Testament era is the realm of magic and divination. Magical beliefs and practices were a part of all religious traditions. . . .
>
> Magic represented a method of manipulating good and evil spirits to lend help or bring harm. Magical formulas could be used for such things as attracting a lover or winning a chariot race. Black magic, or sorcery, involved summoning spirits to accomplish all kinds of evil deeds. Curses could be placed, competitors subdued, and enemies retrained.[4]

These practices naturally left the door open to the demonic world. It could be that Mary Magdalene either participated in or was influenced by these beliefs. The fact that seven demons were cast out of her (Mark 16:9; Luke 8:2) indicates that she must have been actively involved with the powers of darkness to some degree.

We do not know what characteristics of demon possession Mary manifested, but chances are it was quite obvious to those around her that something was desperately wrong. The most vivid description of multiple demon possession in the Gospels is of a man from the region of the Gerasenes who met Jesus on the shores of the Sea of Galilee:[5]

> This man lived in the tombs, and no one could bind him any more, not even with a chain. For he had often been chained hand and foot, but he tore the chains apart and broke the irons on his feet. No one was strong enough to subdue him. Night and day among the tombs and in the hills he would cry out and cut himself with stones.
>
> Mark 5:3–5 NIV

This is a picture of a man who was in unspeakable agony and a community who greatly feared him. It could be that Mary Magdalene experienced some of these same horrors. However it was, there is little doubt that her release from bondage was dramatic and life-changing, and her gratitude was immediately manifested by her actions. Luke shows her quickly moving from a slave of Satan to a servant of Christ (Luke 8:3).

The Discipleship of Mary Magdalene

There are two key angles we want to explore in terms of Mary's discipleship. The first is her role as one who traveled with Jesus and his disciples, supporting them out of her own means (Luke 8:3). The second is her significant role among the other traveling women.

Witherington makes some keen observations concerning these women who traveled with Jesus. He points out the uniqueness of their mission and how their traditional roles as providers are given new significance in their roles as Christ's disciples:

> Luke 8:1–3 stands in contrast to its historical context in rabbinic Judaism in other regards as well. For a Jewish woman to leave home and travel with a rabbi was not only unheard of, it was scandalous. Even more scandalous was the fact that women, both respectable and not, were among Jesus' traveling companions. Yet it was apparently an intended part of His ministry for women to benefit from His teaching (cf. Luke 10:38–42) and healing.
>
> Luke intends us to understand that these three women were only the most prominent among the [other] women that followed Jesus. Luke indicates that Jesus' actions in behalf of these women freed them to serve both Him and the disciples. Though it was uncommon or unknown for women to be traveling disciples of a rabbi, it was not uncommon for women to support rabbis and their disciples out of their own money. . . .
>
> What is unique about the actions of Jesus' women followers is that the traditional roles of hospitality and service are seen by them as a way to serve not only the physical family but also the family of faith. Being Jesus' disciples did not lead these women to abandon their traditional roles in regard to preparing food, serving, etc. Rather, it gave these roles new significance and importance, for now they could be used to serve the Master and the family of faith. The transformation of these women involved not only assuming new discipleship roles, but also resuming their traditional roles for a new purpose.[6]

Mary, Joanna, Susanna, and the other women were serving Jesus in traditional roles, but the discipleship angle set their services in an entirely new dimension. Christ did not treat them as less important because they served him in this capacity. They were apparently taught by him, as were the male disciples, and were also witnesses to his miracles.

It seems that these women were not excluded from any aspect of Christ's ministry except they were not named apostles, but this does not make them any less significant. They played a very important role in Christ's mission. These faithful women supported Jesus and the Twelve "out of their own means" (Luke 8:3 NIV).

It is safe to say that if it wasn't for their support, Christ's ministry would have been greatly hindered. He probably could not have traveled so extensively if it wasn't for their faithful, consistent service. They were the backbone of his ministry.

As we shall see, however, these women were not destined to work exclusively behind the scenes. The death and resurrection of their Master soon ushered them to the forefront, while their male counterparts quickly faded into the background. These traveling female disciples were among the first to witness the risen Christ.

It is important to point out that whether these women were in the shadows or out in front, they proved themselves to be faithful, loyal disciples. They are outstanding models of servanthood. Christ had set them free, and they turned out to be some of his most committed disciples. As such, they are worthy to be recognized.

As for the significance of Mary Magdalene's role among the other women, her name always appears first whenever the women are listed. This is probably because she, much like Peter, was considered the leader. In fact, Luke spotlights Mary, Joanna, and Susanna among the women much as Peter, James, and John are often the focus among the Twelve.

The three women are probably emphasized because the power of the gospel was dramatically displayed in their lives through healing. However, it is also possible that Luke drew special attention to them because of their leadership roles among the other women. Mary Magdalene is the dominant one among the three. The comparison and contrast between her and Peter will become even more clear at the scenes of the cross and tomb of Christ. Her unique role as the very first to witness and tell of the risen Christ gives her a special place in salvation history and in the outworking of these extraordinary events.

Gospel Portraits of Mary Magdalene at the Cross and Tomb

Matthew's Portrayal

In Matthew's Gospel the courage of Mary Magdalene and the other women is set in stark contrast to the unbelief of the Jewish leaders and the absence of the Eleven. Table 2, page 22, shows the inverted structure of Matthew 27:50–28:20. To get a clear picture of how prominent Mary Magdalene was at the cross and tomb, notice that in each case that the women are mentioned, Mary Magdalene is named first (27:56, 61; 28:1).

Mary Magdalene is depicted by Matthew as the one who leads the women in witnessing these remarkable events. Witherington points out, "It is striking that all four Gospels agree in listing Mary of Magdala. . . . In every instance in the Gospels where women followers of Jesus are mentioned, Mary Magdalene's name is placed first (except in John 19:25 where there is a special interest in Jesus' mother). Mary Magdalene's first place was not only because of her loyalty to Jesus or notable service, but also (and perhaps primarily) because of her witness about the risen Lord."[7]

The significance of Mary Magdalene's witness of the risen Christ will be brought to light in John's portrayal of her, but it is Matthew who gives the most focused attention to her courage. She was boldly present at the cross and tomb despite the possible consequences.

Mark's Portrayal

As was pointed out in chapter 2, Matthew's and Mark's passion accounts are more similar than they are different. Still, Mark sheds further light on the steadfastness of Mary Magdalene and the other women disciples at the cross and tomb.

In his descriptive passion account, Mary Magdalene and the others stand out as Jesus' only faithful followers in the midst of hostile enemies. Mark also stresses that these women were afraid and troubled by what they witnessed, which makes it even more remarkable that they remained on the scene as long as they did.

A chiasm of Mark 15:12–16:8 (see table 3, page 25) contrasts well Mary Magdalene's loyalty to Jesus with the hostility of his enemies. Notice again that in each case where the women are mentioned (Mark 15:40, 47; 16:1), Mary Magdalene is the first one named.

The longer ending of Mark (Mark 16:9–20)[8] confirms that Mary told the male disciples that the Lord had risen, but they did not believe her (Mark 16:11). This reinforces Mark's apparent emphasis on the steadfastness of the women disciples. They were fearful, but they stood strong in the face of the most intense hostility.

Luke's Portrayal

Matthew portrays Mary and the other women as courageous disciples. Mark focuses on their loyalty and steadfastness as disciples. Luke pictures Mary and the others as disciples of amazing faith. The chiastic structure found in Luke 23:54–24:49 features them at the center and draws explicit attention to their remarkable faith (see table 5, page 28).

The mirroring ideas presented in Luke 23:54–24:49 clearly reveal that the apostles and the two disciples on the Emmaus road had to *see* in order to believe. In this scene, the women were the only ones to exercise faith and believe solely on the angel's testimony (Luke 24:4–9). Tucker and Liefeld further elucidate their extraordinary role:

> The point is not simply that the women were there [at the tomb]; it is rather that they were commissioned to tell. But immediately they encountered a problem, and this problem makes the commission all the more striking. Luke reports that when the other disciples heard the report of the women, "they did not believe the women, because their words seemed to them like nonsense" (Luke 24:11 NIV). Luke's record is not a put-down of the women, as some have supposed. On the contrary, if anything, it is a put-down of the men who failed to believe them. But it is not certain that the men disbelieved because the messengers were women. No one seemed disposed to believe the Resurrection facts at first. This makes the belief and boldness of the women all the more significant.[9]

John's Portrayal

Nowhere is Mary Magdalene's role as a faithful witness to the risen Christ more clearly seen than in John's Gospel. His passion narrative is unique in at least two ways. First, he focuses exclusively on Mary as the first to witness and tell about Christ's resurrection (John 20:10–18). Second, he does not use a chiastic structure.[10]

What the apostle John does is give us a more intimate look at the conversation that took place between Jesus and Mary (John 20:15–17). While Mary stood at the tomb crying, Jesus approached her, but she did not recognize that it was Jesus until he spoke her name. Elizabeth Tetlow offers an interesting perspective on this scene:

When he called her by name, "Mary," she recognized who he was. In an earlier discourse in John 10 the fourth evangelist presented Jesus speaking about himself in the image of the good shepherd and of his disciples as sheep. . . . In the good shepherd passage the shepherd's "own" recognize him because he calls them by name. In the resurrection narrative it was when Jesus called Mary by name that she recognized him. . . .
When he called her by name, she recognized him and believed. According to johannine theology this doubly confirmed her discipleship: it portrayed her as one of Jesus' own and as believing, both of which were essential for the true disciple. Then she was given the apostolic commission by the risen Jesus. She is portrayed in the following verse as fulfilling this mission by pronouncing the standard formula of the apostolic proclamation of the resurrection: "I have seen the Lord."[11]

Tetlow rightly contends that this passage confirms Mary Magdalene as a true disciple. She also points out that the apostle John is essentially portraying Mary as an "apostle to the apostles." She preaches the resurrection to the ones Christ commissions to preach a few verses later (John 20:21). But Jesus had to send her before he could send them.

Hence, in John's portrayal, the Great Commission is given (and acted on) in seminal form by Mary Magdalene. This is an amazing thing when we consider again where she came from. She was the one who was possessed by seven demons. She was enslaved to Satan and held captive to evil. Her life was characterized by darkness and gloom.

Now we have come to know Mary Magdalene as a loyal servant of Christ and the faithful first witness of his resurrection. She was the first one entrusted with the glorious news and the first one to proclaim it.

The Legacy of Mary Magdalene

Mary Magdalene was a faithful, loyal disciple of Jesus Christ. She moved from a slave of darkness to a servant of the Light. She teaches us that our past need not hinder us on the path to discipleship.[12] As Jesus released her from bondage, so he releases us to freely serve him.

Mary also teaches us that being a faithful witness involves more than a mere verbal proclamation. It is a life characterized by service and devotion to the Master.

Five

MARY AND MARTHA

Through the Thick and Thin of Life

Most of us are probably familiar with the expression: "Actions speak louder than words." The meaning of the phrase is clear. We generally judge the character and sincerity of people by what they *do* rather than by what they *say*.

For instance, when trouble comes our way and we find ourselves in need, we call on our friends to stand by our side. If they come through for us, we judge them to be true and loyal friends. If, on the other hand, they do not come to our aid, we do not consider them to be genuine friends. Either way, it was their actions (or lack thereof), much more than their words, that finally determined our view of their character. People's actions can have a tremendous impact on us. So much so that their words pale in comparison.

Also, we usually remember people by their actions much more clearly than we remember them by their words. This is especially true when we think of Mary and Martha, whose actions have spoken louder than their words down through the centuries.

Disciples in Action

Mary and Martha were faithful and loyal friends of Jesus, who stuck by him through the thick and thin of life, but they were also genuine disciples. This will become abundantly clear as we study their lives more closely. As faithful friends and loyal disciples of Jesus, they will teach us about honesty, integrity, and service. We will learn that they were two drastically different personalities, who expressed their discipleship in different ways.

Their distinct learning processes come out most clearly in the infamous scene recorded in Luke 10:38–42. Here we find Martha distracted by preparations to serve Jesus and Mary sitting at his feet. In this particular situation, Mary did indeed choose the better action (v. 42). She was sitting at the feet of Jesus, learning from him. Unquestionably, Mary is viewed here in the role of a disciple.[1] This should not distract us, however, from also seeing Martha in the position of a disciple. Since she is the primary focus of this passage, we must point out that this situation was very much a learning experience for her also.

Witherington greatly helps us to understand Martha in this light. He points out how Luke's literary arrangement and the overall content of this scene work together to show what Martha needed to learn (which every disciple of Jesus should take to heart). He also gives invaluable insight into Mary's example of discipleship:

> The Lucan story is a brief vignette sandwiched between two crucial sections—the Good Samaritan and the Lord's Prayer. It seems possible to see a purpose and progression in this arrangement: the Good Samaritan parable (10:25–37) gives

an example of how to serve and love one's neighbor, Luke 10:38–42 teaches that the "one thing necessary" is not first service, but listening to and learning from Jesus (allowing Jesus to serve us), and the Lord's Prayer (11:1–4) gives an example of what is to be heard and learned from Jesus. . . .

Though this story primarily focuses on Martha and what she must learn about "the one thing necessary," Mary appears to know already, for she "was listening to his word." . . . The use of the phrase "to sit at the feet of" in 10:39 is significant since there is evidence that this is a technical formula meaning "to be a disciple of." If so, then Luke is intimating to his audience that Mary is a disciple and as such her behaviour is to be emulated. . . .

It is possible that Martha's behaviour is atypical and reflects her desire and willingness to serve Jesus, even if it meant assuming a servant's role. . . . Rather than serving quietly without complaint, she vents her feelings by accusing Jesus of not caring, and indirectly accusing Mary of neglecting her when she needed help. . . . Jesus defends Mary's right to learn from Him and says this is the crucial thing for those who wish to serve Him. Jesus makes clear that for women as well as men, one's primary task is to be a proper disciple; only in that context can one be a proper hostess.[2]

According to Witherington's explanation of this passage, this turned out to be a significant event in Martha's life. She could choose to learn from Christ's words and Mary's example, or she could continue to serve him in her own way. John 11:1–44 and 12:2 clearly reveal that Martha chose the former, but she had to learn the hard way.

This particular passage gives us a hint of Mary's and Martha's distinct learning styles. It seems that it was generally easier for Mary to submit herself to Jesus and learn from him. For Martha, this process took a little longer. It apparently took some confrontation to encourage her to change her ways. But, as we shall see, Martha eventually proved herself to be every bit the disciple her sister was.

Luke 10:38–42 indeed portrays Mary as the better example of discipleship. But here we can also learn from Martha, whose desire and eagerness to serve Jesus is also worthy to be emulated.

Through Death to Discipleship

The account of Lazarus's death and resurrection in John 11 witnesses to the perplexing truth that God's timing is often mysterious. However it also showcases Martha's growth as a disciple. In John 11 both Mary and Martha teach us many compelling aspects of discipleship through how they deal with their loss and grief.

Mary, Martha, and Lazarus were intimate friends and disciples of Jesus. Even so, he did not come right away when he heard of Lazarus's illness. Wasn't he concerned about these people who were so dear to him?

As far as Mary and Martha knew, Jesus was too late. Their brother was dead and so was their hope. It seemed as though their Lord had failed them. But they understood only half of the picture. Like the man who was born blind (John 9:1–3), this loss was orchestrated for a divine purpose. This tragedy would bring glory to the Son of God (John 11:4).

In keeping with John's overall purpose (20:30–31), this seventh and greatest sign[3] of the fourth Gospel would further manifest Christ's deity so that the world might believe in him. The Son of God would now demonstrate his power over death.

Lazarus's resurrection evoked faith in some people, but it also hardened many others (11:45–46). In their fury to suppress the truth, the Pharisees heightened their opposition to Christ. Consequently this miraculous event led to

Jesus' death and resurrection, which was the ultimate witness to his divine glory.

However, Mary and Martha could not initially comprehend this heavenly plan. They were not able to see past their tears. Blinded by the pain of their loss, they could experience only the here and now. Their faith was being severely tested.

Mary and Martha's secure, predictable lives in Bethany were shattered by the mysterious absence of their Lord during their time of greatest need. They stayed close to their home, trying to make sense of their brother's untimely death. They waited. Would Jesus *ever* come?

A Day Late—A Life Short

In many ways, it was a day much like any other. The sun came up and burned away the damp morning dew that was blanketing the ground. The villagers scurried about on the stone-paved street, occupied with their daily tasks. Many of them were too busy to notice the beautiful, blossoming almond trees, the fruitful, green fig trees, or the ripe olive trees, which testified to God's favor. Yes, it was a normal day in Bethany . . . except for one thing. Lazarus was on his deathbed.

Lazarus, his sisters, and Jesus were close friends. Love seemed to have characterized their relationship (John 11:3, 5). The siblings readily opened their home to Jesus when his ministry brought him to Jerusalem (Luke 10:38). In fact, he probably spent his last week on earth at their home (Matt. 21:17). Mary, Martha, and Lazarus held a special place in our Lord's heart. The little town of Bethany was also meaningful to him, for he spent a significant amount of time there.[4]

Situated on the southeastern slope of the Mount of Olives, Bethany was a lonely village. Bethany (the name means "place of unripe figs" or "house of the afflicted one"[5]) was known as "the house of misery" because of the invalids and outcasts who gathered there.[6]

Yet people Jesus loved and associated with resided in this grievous little village. It is both striking and comforting to know that he preferred to visit among the needy people of Bethany rather than among those who were well-off in Jerusalem (e.g., the Pharisees).

The call for help went out to Jesus from this humble little town: "Lord, the one you love is sick" (John 11:3 NIV). The message was urgent and precise, and Mary and Martha were certainly expecting a quick response from their Lord. They knew that Jesus was only about a day's journey from Bethany.[7] But when three days had passed and he still hadn't arrived, all hope began to drain from their lives.

The apostle John makes it clear that Jesus loved Mary, Martha, and Lazarus very much (11:3, 5). His deliberate delay did not reflect a lack of concern for his beloved friends; it was for a much greater purpose (11:4). But how were Mary and Martha interpreting their Lord's absence? Remember, they had no idea that the Son of God was about to be glorified through his resurrection of their brother. All they knew was what they were experiencing: Lazarus was dead and Jesus was nowhere to be found!

Finally, though, Jesus did arrive. But by then Lazarus had been dead for four days. Feelings of anger and disappointment emerged from Martha's heart as she hurried to meet Jesus just outside the village. She said: "Lord, if you had been here, my brother would not have died" (11:21). Her eyes undoubtedly revealed to Jesus the hurt and confusion lodged deep in her soul.

Faith in Spite of Pain

What is also noteworthy about this entire interaction between Jesus and Martha (11:21–27) is what it reveals about her as a disciple. In their conversation Jesus made the astounding proclamation: "I am the resurrection and the life. He who believes in me will live, even though he dies; and whoever lives and believes in me will never die. Do you believe this?" (John 11:25–26 NIV).[8]

Martha made an equally astounding proclamation when she said: "Yes, Lord, . . . I believe that you are the Christ, the Son of God, who was to come into the world" (11:27 NIV). This amazing statement shows that Martha, like her sister, Mary, must have spent time at the Master's feet (Luke 10:39). Tetlow and Witherington make some extraordinary comments on the significance of Martha's proclamation:

> The gospel of John begins and ends with the proclamation of Jesus as the Messiah and the Son of God. The solemn confession of Martha that Jesus is Messiah and Son of God is the climactic midpoint of the gospel. In this scene the most important role of discipleship according to johannine theology, that of proclamation of Jesus' true identity, is given to a woman.[9]

> By giving his audience a story in which a woman is the recipient of one of Jesus' most profound and direct statements about Himself, and in which a woman makes a heartfelt and accurate response to Jesus' declarations, the Fourth Evangelist intimates that women have the right to be taught even the mysteries of the faith, and that they are capable of responding in faith with an accurate confession. In short, they are capable of being full-fledge disciples of Jesus.[10]

What an incredible testimony to Martha's discipleship! Her declaration stands as a witness to her great learning. Her overall conversation with Jesus also reflects that she was not afraid to be honest with him, even when that honesty could have possibly hurt their relationship.

Turning to Mary, we find that she again manifests her quieter nature by staying home when she heard of the Lord's arrival. That does not mean, however, that she was not filled with the same anguish displayed by Martha. When she finally saw Jesus, she echoed her sister's exact words, "Lord, if You had been here, my brother would not have died" (John 11:32).

In four days of waiting, both Mary and Martha probably had uttered this disheartening statement to one another many times. The waiting had taken its toll. Distraught and bewildered, they both let him know immediately what was in their hearts.

However, it is obvious that this excruciating trial did not destroy their faith in Christ. Though expressed in different ways, Mary and Martha's commitment to him as disciples was clearly evident. Martha communicated it verbally: "But I know that even now God will give you whatever you ask" (11:22 NIV). Mary conveyed her reverent devotion nonverbally: "When Mary reached the place where Jesus was and saw him, she fell at his feet" (11:32 NIV).

Hence, as angry and disappointed as their feelings toward Christ were at that point, that did not connote a lack of faith. On the contrary, their emotions revealed their dedication to him because they showed the depth of their relationship with him.

Their relationship with Jesus was not shallow. Mary and Martha were able to speak the truth about how they felt, and Jesus accepted their honest feelings. Consequently, his grace and truth came together once again to bring them hope and healing.

Jesus gave them grace by listening to them, feeling with them, and responding to their need. He listened on two levels: He heard their words and their feelings. His display of emotions indicate that both his ears and his heart were open to them. Sharing in their overwhelming grief, he felt their loss deeply and wept with them (11:33–35).

Christ's emotions were spontaneous and free. Though he knew exactly what the outcome was going to be, he was

still moved to weep with his beloved friends over the death
of their brother. He acknowledged their loss; he did not
view their tears as a lack of faith. His grace was then bal-
anced by the truth about the situation. The truth was that this heart-wrenching loss was sover-
eignly designed by the Lord (11:4, 15, 40, 45). Jesus was
not guilty of bad timing. The glory of God was going to be
displayed in this tragedy. The resurrection of Lazarus would
strengthen their faith and move the world to believe in
Christ. Their pain would not be in vain. As disciples, Mary and Martha held tenaciously to their
faith, and the truth was revealed to them. They saw the
glory of God. They now understood his ultimate purpose
for their trial. They witnessed an incredible miracle that
confirmed a universal truth: God has the power to raise the
dead! He can transform a hopeless predicament into a glorious victory. Tragedy is an opportunity for God to manifest his sovereignty, power, and love.

Learning from Mary and Martha

Several crucial principles related to discipleship can be
gleaned from John 11:

1. *God is in sovereign control.* He was aware of Lazarus's
situation and knew exactly what he was going to do. As odd
as it seems sometimes, God, in his perfection, is not even
capable of bad timing. He allowed Lazarus's death to take
place because he had a greater plan (John 11:4). As a result,
Mary and Martha learned volumes about the sovereignty
of God.

If you are experiencing loss or pain in your life, I encourage you to find comfort in his sovereignty. He is aware of
your unique circumstance. He is present with you. He has
allowed you to experience your pain for a purpose. He is in
sovereign control. This is not a dry doctrine that is important only for high-minded theologians. There is great con-

solation in this divine truth. He will not be late to meet you in your time of great need.

2. *On the basis of a trusting relationship with him, God hears and accepts our honest feelings.* Mary and Martha were secure enough in their discipleship relationship with Christ to be honest with him. If they had attempted to hide their true feelings, it would have indicated a lack of trust. The silence would have put a wedge in their close relationship. But they took a risk and learned that their Lord accepted both the good and the bad in them. While the text is silent on the matter, Jesus' willingness to accept them as they were undoubtedly brought them closer together in the time ahead.

You can also trust God with your true feelings, even if you feel angry with him for your circumstances. Allow the Lord of Love to know who you really are. He already knows everything about you: the good and the bad. A reluctance to share the truth about yourself can stifle your discipleship relationship with him. He can be trusted with all of your feelings. Take the risk and you will discover the compassionate and loving Savior waiting to embrace every part of you. He is safe. Honesty leads to a deeper, more secure relationship with him.

3. *God feels the pain of our overwhelming trials along with us.* Jesus did not interpret Mary and Martha's feelings as a lack of faith. He compassionately understood their grief and wept with them. We can expect a similar loving response from our Lord.

The Lord identifies with you in your distress. He does not condemn your feelings. He gave you your feelings and emotions. Whether it was your sin or the sins committed against you that are causing your sorrow, the God of all mercy feels it along with you.

If your pain is the result of your own sin, then ask for God's forgiveness, mercy, and understanding. You can know that your Redeemer lives to make you whole and restore you to himself.

4. *Sometimes God allows our needs to go unmet temporarily, which results in deep pain.* But he can bring about a greater good through the experience for his glory and the strengthening of our faith. Mary and Martha needed Jesus to heal their sick brother. The need was not fulfilled, and it resulted in his death. Although they were not aware of it, Jesus planned for a greater good to come out of this loss. He was able to demonstrate his power over the grave.

A deep pain in my own life has been the loss of my childhood. Because of the utter chaos and dysfunction in my family, my emotional needs were not met. I mourn for my lost childhood, but I cannot redeem it. A sense of emptiness and loss will always be present in this life.

However, God is meeting my deep emotional needs in some of the relationships I have today. My husband, my church, a special small group, and a few close friends have helped to fill the destitute places in my heart. I trust that the Lord had good reasons for allowing these childhood needs to go unsatisfied. I am confident that one day, if not until eternity, I will understand his purposes.

Do you feel the pain of unmet needs? Have you lost a loved one to death? Has sin in your family robbed you of your childhood? Has an abortion left you feeling empty, guilty, and alone? The misery of those losses are devastating. But the Lord understands your grief. Whether in this life or in eternity, God says, "I will make up to you for the years that the swarming locust has eaten" (Joel 2:25). God cares about your needs. He has not forsaken you. Don't stop believing in him. Though you don't understand what it is yet, the Lord is bringing about a greater good through your pain.[11]

As was clearly seen in the lives of Mary and Martha, faith is absolutely necessary to grow as disciples. Faith did not prevent them from experiencing pain and loss, but it enabled them to reach out to Christ in their time of need (John 11:3). Jesus honored their faith. He interacted with them on the basis of their loving and trusting relationship. He drew near and embraced them with his grace and truth. This same relationship with the living Christ is still available to us today. However, because he is not physically present, faith can be much more difficult for us. As we have trusted him for our eternal salvation, so we must believe that he will take us on through the stages of discipleship. The story of Lazarus is an example of Jesus' willingness to be there for us in times of great emotional distress. He ministers to us through his Spirit and his body, the church. We can depend on him. But like Mary and Martha, we must learn to stay close to the Lord.

God's grace and truth can carry us through the storms of life and give us wholeness in spite of the great losses we have endured. He brings life out of death. He draws the good out of the bad. In a very real sense, he strips us of our grave clothes and adorns us in robes of righteousness.

A Final Scene at Bethany

This study of Mary and Martha has taught us many valuable aspects in regard to women as Christ's disciples. But one of the most outstanding lessons we can learn from their lives has yet to be thoroughly discussed. What is that lesson? Maturity often comes through extreme adversity. The ordeal of their brother's death and the subsequent encounter with Jesus in John 12 caused Mary and Martha to grow as his disciples.

The last time we see Mary and Martha is at their home in Bethany. It is in the context of a dinner given for their honored guest, Jesus, that their maturity as disciples is beautifully displayed (John 12:1–3). As we would naturally expect, Mary and Martha expressed their growth in different ways. Their actions clearly reflect their unique personalities.

For the first time, though, we see Mary as the focus of a particular scene. Indeed, what she does is extremely significant and worthy to be spotlighted. Her act of devotion, the anointing of Jesus for burial, shows her tremendous understanding of his mission. Her insight is starkly contrasted with the other disciples' failure to understand:

It was not until after the Resurrection that the [other] disciples were able to understand that the Cross had to precede the crown. But one disciple did seem to understand. Six days before the final Passover, Jesus went to the familiar home at Bethany where Lazarus, Mary, and Martha lived. . . . Mary took "about a pint of pure nard, an expensive perfume; she poured it on Jesus' feet and wiped his feet with her hair." . . . It is hard to escape the conclusion that this woman had a deeper understanding of the impending cross than did Jesus' male disciples.[12]

What Mary learned at the feet of Jesus and what she witnessed of his power to raise her brother from the dead brought her to maturity. Her theological insight and sacrificial service stand as a solid witness to her growth as a disciple.

But what about Martha?[13] What evidence is there in this passage that she grew as a disciple? The evidence of her maturity is actually best seen in what is *not* written. Witherington explains:

In John 12 there are no complaints by Martha and no hint of a rebuke to Martha—she serves quietly. . . . In comparing the portraits of Martha in Luke 10 and John 12, we note that Martha appears in the same role in both cases. . . . Luke 10 makes it clear that a woman must first orientate her priorities so that the good portion comes first, being the one thing necessary. Having her priorities straight (as in John 12) she can assume a role that servants usually performed. This role is given new significance as a means of serving the Master and manifesting discipleship to and love for Him.[14]

Both Mary and Martha stand out as shining examples of servanthood and discipleship. From beginning to end their actions have spoken louder than their words. In fact, the very last time we see Mary and Martha in John 12, their words are not even recorded—only their actions. Maybe there is a lesson for us in this as well.

Six

THE SAMARITAN WOMAN

Unacceptable yet Astute

She is best known not by her name but by her lifestyle. In fact, we don't even know her name. Normally it would not be such a bad thing to be remembered by how you lived—if you lived in a righteous manner. But this is clearly not the case with this particular woman. She is well remembered for a shoddy lifestyle.

Her familiar story is found in the Gospel of John. During Christ's earthly ministry, he came in contact with this woman under the most unusual circumstances. This was a woman who, by reason of her unethical lifestyle, was deemed unacceptable by those around her. She was the type of woman people went out of their way to avoid.

John simply refers to her as the Samaritan woman (John 4). Perhaps by leaving her unnamed, the apostle is attempting to give his audience a deeper impression of her unworthiness. Or it could be that he kept her anonymous to focus more on her unacceptable condition.

Whatever the reason, we shall soon see that there was considerably more to this woman than meets the eye. Yes, she did have a troublesome, immoral background. Thus we naturally would not expect that a woman of such questionable character could provide an example of anything good. But Christ brought out the best in the Samaritan woman. In the process of unveiling her dark side (John 4:17), he brought to light a very bright woman. Underneath the layers of shame and guilt lay intelligence and discernment. Christ unearthed for himself an astute disciple.

It is possible that you come from a background similar to that of the Samaritan woman. You may be known, even in your own church, by a past bad reputation. You may know all too intimately what it is like to feel unworthy and unacceptable.

Whether or not you can identify with any of these feelings, we offer you a message of hope and inspiration from the life of the Samaritan woman. Christ saw more in her than just sin and degradation. He saw a potential fruitful disciple, and he gave her a chance to believe in him. She, in turn, broke from the religious traditions of her people and her own personal lifestyle and followed him on the path of discipleship.

From an applicational standpoint, the fact that John even recorded Christ's encounter with this unnamed, unacceptable Samaritan woman communicates a powerful message: Women, even the most unsuitable ones, have more to offer than is apparent on the surface and are not excluded from Christ's call to discipleship.[1] Jesus' ministry was revolutionary in many ways but it was especially so with regard to women.

A Worthy Candidate for Discipleship

As we have seen in the previous chapters, Jesus did not avoid women or look down on them. On the contrary, with every meeting he gave them an equal opportunity to believe and to become his disciples. This is clearly seen in his encounter with the Samaritan woman.

From the outset, this potential disciple had two strikes against her: her gender and her lifestyle. Christ decisively broke through those barriers and brought out the best in her, and she responded to his call to discipleship. Unfortunately the Scriptures do not give us a detailed description of her life after her encounter with Christ.

However, by virtue of the fact that she so diligently, yet cautiously, responded to Christ's call, she stands as a noble example of an astute and discerning female disciple. As we briefly examine her life, it will become apparent that even the most seemingly unsuitable woman has something to offer and can make a valuable contribution to the Kingdom of God.

The apostle John begins his discussion of Christ's encounter with the Samaritan woman with some interesting background information.[2] This is a significant, yet often overlooked, angle to the entire story. He informs us:

> The Pharisees heard that Jesus was gaining and baptizing more disciples than John, although in fact it was not Jesus who baptized, but his disciples. When the Lord learned of this, he left Judea and went back once more to Galilee.
>
> John 4:1–3 NIV

In the previous section (John 3:22–36), the apostle tells how Jesus' ministry began to overshadow the ministry of

John the Baptist. Some of John's disciples told him that
Jesus was baptizing and that "everyone is going to him"
(v. 26 NIV). John the Baptist informed his concerned disciples that this turn of events was ordained in eternity: "He
must become greater; I must become less" (v. 30 NIV).

With this important information on the ministry of John
the Baptist in the background, the apostle John sets the
stage for the scene with the Samaritan woman by bringing
Jesus' discipleship ministry to the forefront. Thus it is no
accident that the idea of discipleship precedes Christ's
encounter with the Samaritan woman.

The implication that can be drawn from John's introduction is that Jesus was now bringing his discipleship ministry into Samaria. In fact, "the words 'had to' translate an
expression of necessity."[3] It is not as if Jesus just chose to
go through Samaria. It's more like he was under divine compulsion to journey through there.[4]

This wording gives further support to the idea that Jesus
was going through Samaria for the set purpose to make disciples. A Samaritan woman with a shoddy background
would be the firstfruit of his labor there. She would be the
one to spread the word throughout her village that the Messiah had come (John 4:29).

A Divine Appointment

Most everything about Christ's meeting with the Samaritan woman was unusual. It was unusual for a Jew to travel
through Samaria, even though it was the shortest route
between Jerusalem and Galilee. "Many Jews would not travel
by that road, for they regarded any contact with Samaritans
as defiling."[5] Because the Samaritans were half-breeds, they
were considered unclean by the Jewish people.[6]

Jesus and his disciples arrived at Jacob's well in the little
Samaritan village called Sychar about noon (the "sixth

hour," John 4:5–6). He sent his disciples into town to buy
some food while he rested at the well. Not long after that
the Samaritan woman came to draw water (vv. 7–8). It was
unusual for a woman both to draw water at midday and to
do so by herself. Keener points out that "the local women
would not come to draw water in the midday heat, but this
woman had to do so, because she had to come alone. . . .
That this Samaritan woman comes to the well alone rather
than in the company of other women probably indicates
that the rest of the women of Sychar did not like her."[7]

It was highly unusual for a man to speak to a woman in
public, but it was even more peculiar that a Jewish man
would speak to a Samaritan woman (v. 9). Keener gives us
more insight into this situation: "Although Jewish teachers warned against talking much with women in general,
they would have especially avoided Samaritan women, who,
they declared, were unclean from birth."[8]

All of these peculiarities give further support to the idea
that this was a divinely appointed meeting. Jesus *had* to go
through Samaria. The woman *had* to draw water by herself at midday. The Samaritan woman was keenly aware of
her need for water but she was soon to learn that the well
could only meet her need to a point.

Pursuing Water—Receiving Living Water

It can be safely said that the Samaritan woman's journey to discipleship began with her desire to meet a personal physical need. When she went out to satisfy that need
for water, she was struck with the reality that her *real* need
was spiritual and much deeper than she originally thought
(John 4:10). Her real need, however, was not within her
power to satisfy.

That real spiritual need could only be met by the Lord
of Life. All she had to do was to receive the "living water"

(v. 10) Jesus freely offered her and it would quench her thirst forever. In fact, his water, which was spiritual in nature, would well up in her to eternal life (vv. 13–14).[9]

Most of us have had this kind of experience at one time or another. We set out to meet a legitimate personal need only to find the Lord standing there offering to us what we *really* need. It's not necessarily wrong to pursue a personal need or goal, especially if it enhances our growth as a disciple. But we must, at the same time, be willing to receive from the Lord what we cannot attain on our own.

The problem is we often find it much easier to pursue something to satisfy our needs than to receive from the Lord what we really need. We like to be in control. We can learn from this initial encounter between Christ and the Samaritan woman: Discipleship is a pursuit, but we must also have the ability to receive.

As salvation is a gift, so discipleship, in many ways, is also a gift. We must be open to receive spiritual sustenance from the Lord to progress on the path to discipleship. Sometimes, as was the case with the Samaritan woman, we are not willing to receive until the destitute part of our heart is revealed.

Exposed and Emerging into the Path of Discipleship

"The woman said to him, 'Sir, give me this water so that I won't get thirsty and have to keep coming here to draw water.' He told her, 'Go, call your husband and come back'" (John 4:15–16 NIV). In examining this exchange between Christ and the Samaritan woman, a natural question might be: What does one statement have to do with the other?

She is finally willing to receive from Jesus, and he, in turn, tells her to go get her husband. This is the exact opposite of what we saw in the previous section. The fact is Christ was in pursuit of her and wished to expose her sin so that she might come to believe in him. She promptly informed him that she had no husband (v. 17).

With that confession, Christ supernaturally unveiled her sordid personal history. Her previous failed relationships and her current adulterous one lay exposed before them (vv. 17–18), but what was truly exposed was her need for "living water" (v. 10). She indeed had a thirst that was much deeper than a physical one, and only he could provide the means to quench it.

The Samaritan woman was so astonished by this revelation that she changed the subject: "Sir, . . . I can see that you are a prophet. Our fathers worshiped on this mountain, but you Jews claim that the place where we must worship is in Jerusalem" (vv. 19–20 NIV). Jesus, however, would not be drawn into the age-old debate between the Jews and the Samaritans about the proper place to worship. Instead, he revealed to her a profound truth about the nature of God. God is Spirit and is not confined to any one place. Rather, because of who he is, he desires to be worshiped in spirit and in truth (vv. 21–24). Whether Jew or Samaritan, true worship must come from an open and honest heart—a lesson she was painfully beginning to learn.

What is incredible about this entire scene is that this lowly Samaritan woman is engaging in such deep theological conversation at all. It is at this point that Christ begins to uncover a very bright woman. He had exposed her sin, but in the process something very significant began to emerge.

It is obvious that she was quite knowledgeable about the Samaritan religion and also seemed sincerely interested in hearing Jesus' religious point of view.[10] Evans makes an insightful observation:

> Jesus not only asked the woman for a drink and not only passed the time of day with her, both unusual things in themselves; he also gave her important theological teaching which, by treating her seriously and by responding to

her replies he brought her to understand, even from a very unpromising beginning. Again Jesus saw the woman as an individual; he brought out and dealt with her specific problems. He saw her also as capable of spiritual discernment.[11]

The Samaritan woman not only proved herself capable of spiritual discernment but also showed herself to be a person who thought through the things she was told. She may have had a sordid and shameful past, but that did not render her gullible. Christ took her seriously, and the real person began to emerge. And she went on to become one of his astute and fruitful disciples.

An Astute Disciple

Christ's conversation with the Samaritan woman was abruptly interrupted with the return of the disciples (John 4:27). They were surprised to find him talking with a woman but did not question him about it. Leaving behind her water jar, the woman returned to her village and implored her people, "Come, see a man who told me everything I ever did" (John 4:29 NIV).

It is interesting to note what she said to the people on her return. Christ revealed an abundance of spiritual truth to her in their encounter, namely, the true nature of God and the true nature of worship. But it was the truth about herself that she went back to the village to proclaim. Christ's ability to search her heart seemed to have left a lasting impression.

However, what is truly impressive and revealing about this woman is the subsequent question she posed to her people: "Could this be the Christ?" (John 4:29 NIV). This inquiry shows that she was seriously considering, but not yet completely convinced of, the validity of Jesus' claim to be the long-awaited Christ (Messiah; John 4:25–26).

Though she was thoroughly amazed at his ability to search her heart, she was not going to believe in him so easily.

Tucker and Liefeld shed some light on the significance of her proclamation. They point out that the Samaritan woman was far from gullible, as many would expect. On the contrary, in this scene she proved herself to be quite thoughtful and astute:

> To begin with, although the woman became a "missionary" to the townspeople, her message was not as clear as might appear on the surface of the text. The first part is clear: "Come, see a man who told me everything I ever did." She was quite open in her attitude to her past and present and also to the perception of Jesus. But the next words convey uncertainty: "Could this be the Christ?" The question in the Greek (introduced by the particle, *meti*) suggests considerable uncertainty. While one might like to celebrate this woman's bold confidence in Christ, something else is indicated that could be even more significant. Far from believing easily, or to put it in crass terms, being gullible, as some might (wrongly) expect a woman to be, this woman was cautious about her conclusion. It is not that she was a doubter, for it is remarkable that any Samaritan would on the basis of one conversation even entertain the possibility that the speaker was the Jewish Messiah! She had ventured into the area of faith, willing to break with her own tradition but not rushing headlong and wide-eyed into something she did not understand.[12]

Not only was the Samaritan thoughtful and astute, she was also a risk-taker. Though she was cautious, she was not afraid to consider the possibility that Jesus was the Christ. If what he said was true, it would mean a complete change of lifestyle for her. Everything from personal relationships to the worship of God would have to be transformed. But she seemed willing to take that chance. She showed herself to be a thinking disciple, one who questioned and yet was not afraid to take a step of faith.

It is important to point out that the Samaritan woman's prudence did not hinder her testimony. When the people heard her, they came out to see Jesus (John 4:30). Hence, she played a significant part in many Samaritans coming to faith in Christ.

We first met this woman as a morally inept and unacceptable person, going to the well to draw water for her physical thirst. But we leave her as a discerning disciple, drawing people to Jesus, the source of living water. As his disciple, she became a fruitful proclaimer of the truth.

A Fruitful Witness to the Samaritan People

We know from several passages in the New Testament that Christ's earthly ministry was primarily to the Jews (e.g., Matt. 10:5; Rom. 15:8). However, he did occasionally minister to those of other ethnic backgrounds. These cases usually involved a healing of some kind (e.g., Mark 7:24–30; Luke 7:1–9). There is no indication in the Gospels that the Gentile recipients of his ministry moved beyond the realm of receiving and made other disciples.

This fact makes the account of the Samaritan woman unique. What is so significant about it is that not only did the Samaritan woman come to believe and by implication become a disciple (John 4:1–3), but, as a result of her witness, "many of the Samaritans from that town believed in him" (John 4:39 NIV).

As we stated earlier, she was the firstfruit of Samaria. The ministry to the Samaritan people began with her. When his (male) disciples returned from town bringing him food, Jesus plainly told them he had already been filled (John 4:32). He had been nourished by the fruit he pro-

duced in the Samaritan woman and also by the fruit she
produced for him (John 4:32–38).

When Jesus' puzzled disciples did not understand (John
4:33), he saw this as a teachable moment and gave them a
lesson on sowing and reaping. The fields of Samaria were
ripe for harvest; they needed only to open their eyes and
see (John 4:35). Witherington comments on the significance of this scene:

> The disciples offer food to Him, but Jesus remarks that He
> has a source of nourishment unknown to them, namely,
> bringing this woman to faith and to the point of sharing
> that faith. . . . The disciples, like the woman, misunder-
> stand Jesus' remark about food by thinking merely on a
> physical level. Jesus then speaks metaphorically about
> teaching and witnessing and the fruit it bears when it leads
> people to faith in Him. In verse 35, Jesus tells them that
> they do not need to wait for the harvest time in order to do
> what they were sent to do. They are exhorted, "Open your
> eyes and look at the fields! They are ripe for harvest." Jesus
> clearly distinguishes between the reaper and the sower in
> verse 37. The disciples are to be the reapers Jesus has sent.
> Who then are the [others] of verse 38? Perhaps the most
> likely answer is, Jesus and the Samaritan woman. Jesus has
> sown the Word in her and, in turn, she has sown the word
> in other Samaritans. Thus, the disciples, the reapers, are
> not to suspect the conversation He had with this woman,
> or her witness in the town. Rather, the sowers and reapers
> are to rejoice together. The disciples must not begrudge
> Jesus His source of nourishment, or the woman the nour-
> ishment she has received. They must turn now and see the
> fruit of the evangelistic work of Jesus and the woman.[13]

Witherington makes some excellent observations concerning the evangelistic work of both Jesus and the Samaritan woman. The most important point he makes, though,
concerns the woman's role as a sower of the Word. She was

the first witness to the Samaritan people concerning the works of Jesus.

In this way her role as a disciple is most clearly seen. The most important role of discipleship in Johannine theology is the proclamation of Jesus' true identity.[14] Though she was slow to believe at first, her testimony still bore fruit and her witness stood firm. In this particular passage the woman was functioning as a sower and the other (male) disciples were reapers (John 4:36–38).

By this analogy, Jesus may have been exhorting his male disciples to recognize this woman as an equal disciple and to acknowledge her work as his witness. As Witherington pointed out, the reaper and sower were "to rejoice together." In other words, they were to appreciate each other's work.

In summary, we have learned that the Samaritan woman had more to offer than a broken and sinful lifestyle. She was indeed leading a life of immorality, but Jesus' confrontation unveiled her dark side and revealed a very bright and discerning woman. She eventually received his living waters of eternal life and became one of his fruitful disciples.

The Samaritan woman stands out as one who was not afraid to break with what was familiar (including her sinful lifestyle) and take that vital step of faith. "'The hour is coming and now is' when even women, even Samaritan women, even sinful Samaritan women, may be both members and messengers of this King and His Kingdom."[15]

Part 2

Women Disciples in the Early Church

Seven

TABITHA/DORCAS
A Model Disciple

When the term *model* is used today, most people immediately think of someone who looks much better than average in next season's new clothing. If, for the sake of clarification, you expand the wording to *role model,* the tone of the conversation generally changes quickly and quite dramatically. Many are upset because it is often the most recognizable faces among athletes, musical performers, and the acting profession who are looked up to as the role models of our culture. Sadly, their financial greed, their drug, alcohol, or marital problems, or their general immaturity and insensitivity are spotlighted almost as frequently as their talent or any good qualities.

Of course that does not mean that there are no good role models around to emulate. It's just that such positive models are never as splashy or controversial and thus, in the estimation of the media, not worthy of their prime air time or print space. So it is necessary to be on the lookout to observe such positive role models. It is well worth the extra effort, though, when the healthy example and impact of these typically unassuming people in their individual spheres of influence are thoughtfully considered.

It is regrettable, of course, that so many of the people who need to be exposed to such exemplary role models will not be because these unsung heroes and heroines are laboring steadily and effectively in workaday, even obscure, surroundings. Wouldn't it be wonderful if the spotlight were turned on some of these eminently deserving but humbly unambitious examples?

A Surprising, Spotlighted Figure

The New Testament gives little direct attention to women as role models for discipleship, but there is a striking exception that is very important in the study of women disciples. In Acts 9:36 Luke introduces "a certain disciple named Tabitha (which translated in Greek is called Dorcas)."

The most amazing thing about this wording is not that it is the first clear mention of a woman as a disciple but that it is the *only* direct reference to a woman as a disciple in the New Testament.[1] Certainly this lack of usage is understandable in a patriarchal society where being a disciple of any teacher would have been highly unusual for any Jewish woman. Thus, being called a disciple of Jesus, even with his great concern for women, was almost out of the question.

Yet that does not explain why the exception was made by Luke, and, most strikingly, why Dorcas was that exception, especially since Joppa was hardly a crucial city in the narrative of Acts. There is nothing that is obviously extraordinary about Dorcas's life, except that she was brought back to life by Peter (Acts 9:40–41).

Nor does it explain why Dorcas was included in the select company of being one out of only five individual disciples of Christ who are named in Acts (Ananias, 9:10; Paul, 9:26; Dorcas, 9:36; Timothy, 16:1; Mnason, 21:16). That inclusion becomes even more tantalizing when it is noted that two of the five are Paul and Timothy.

Some explain Dorcas being called a disciple as an off-handed usage, merely parallel to the mention of the believers at Joppa as "the disciples" in 9:38.[2] That could be the case, but it doesn't really come to grips with why it does not occur with key women characters elsewhere in the New Testament. Nor does it answer why Dorcas is the only woman named as a disciple.[3]

Thus, it seems very possible that Luke purposefully included the unique description of Dorcas as disciple to focus a sort of spotlight on her as an unexpected role model for discipleship. If that is the case, the question of why he did this must be answered from Acts 9:36–43 and its careful positioning in Acts, since that is the only passage in which Dorcas is mentioned.

A Crucial Crossroads Context

Sadly, Dorcas is far from being a household name among lay Christians. We would be less likely to overlook Dorcas, however, if we had a sufficient appreciation for the context in which her story is found.

Notice how carefully Luke puts together this section of Acts. The focus on Dorcas in 9:36–43 grows out of the summary statement on the status and expansion of the church in 9:31. Apparently the events focused on until the next summary growth statement in Acts 11:19 are to be taken as significant examples of how the church expanded "throughout all Judea and Galilee and Samaria" (Acts 9:31) in keeping with Christ's Great Commission statement in Acts 1:8.[4]

Interestingly, only three locations in the region are included: Lydda (9:32), Joppa (9:36), and Caesarea (10:1). The sequence indicates that the apostle Peter's ministry was venturing farther and farther away from Jerusalem, toward heavily Gentile territory, even though Peter doesn't seem to be aware of that initially (Acts 10:10–35). Also, in each location only one encounter is described in any detail. That is readily seen by the parallel wording "a certain man named Aeneas" (9:33), "a certain disciple named Tabitha" (9:36), and "a certain man . . . named Cornelius" (10:1).

This three-part development is not often noted, probably because the focus on Cornelius is a lengthy double take: Peter in Caesarea (10:24–48), then back in Jerusalem (11:1–18). But the imbalance in the length of the passages is undoubtedly due to Cornelius being the classic Gentile convert of the Book of Acts (at least up to that point).

A Certain Disciple

The introduction of Dorcas at the beginning of the passage is a change of pace from the scene before: the ministry of Peter in Lydda that included the healing of paralyzed Aeneas (9:32–35). There Peter's travel and arrival in Lydda is mentioned initially. Also, Aeneas is merely called "a certain man," while Dorcas is termed "a certain female disciple." The difference in wording may indicate that Aeneas was not yet a Christian, as is the case with Cornelius (10:1), who is also called "a certain man." That is unclear because there is nothing specific about Aeneas being converted, just a general statement that many in the area of Lydda and Sharon "turned to the Lord" (9:35). By contrast, Cornelius's conversion is described at length (10:39–48).

In any case, the surrounding of the Dorcas passage by the more generally worded references to Aeneas and Cornelius as "a certain man" definitely calls attention to the specific description of Dorcas as "a certain *disciple*." Perhaps there is further emphasis implied in placing Dorcas in this category of disciple that Luke has already defined as requiring great commitment (Luke 14:25–35). In that regard, it is at least plausible that Dorcas is compared as a disciple with Ananias and even Paul in his pre-Antioch ministry, since both are also called a "disciple" in the same chapter before Dorcas (Acts 9:10, 26, 36).

Full of Good Works

After focusing on Dorcas in the narrative by calling her a female disciple, Luke immediately tells us what characterized her discipleship. Unfortunately, neither the NIV nor NASB translations are adequate to discern how this description functions in Acts.

Admittedly we do get the flavor of the astounding concern and generosity of Dorcas in hearing that she "was always doing good and helping the poor" (9:36 NIV). Yet a precise translation of the Greek is even more beneficial in this case: "full of good works and financial generosity to the needy."

Within the book of Acts two other *very* important characters are described by this "full of ___ and ___" construction. The first is the courageous Stephen, who is said to be "full of faith and of the Holy Spirit" (Acts 6:5), then "full of grace and power" (6:8). Later in the book, the great encourager, Barnabas, is described as "full of the Holy Spirit and of faith" in 11:24, merely reversing the word order of 6:5.

At first glance it may seem that the parallels between the description of Dorcas and that of Stephen and Barnabas is either coincidental or, at most, of secondary importance.

However, when background factors regarding Stephen and Barnabas are brought into play, as well as the wider context of the statement about Dorcas, the clear similarity in wording and construction emerges as a strikingly planned echo.

First, with both Stephen and Barnabas, the first description given of each of their ministries has to do with service to needy believers that came about through financial generosity. In the case of Barnabas, it was by giving all the proceeds from the sale of a piece of land (Acts 4:36–37). With Stephen, it was as one of the seven elected by the church in Jerusalem to minister specifically to the needs of the Greek-speaking Jewish widows among them (6:1–6). Interestingly the funding for the work in which Stephen was engaged came from generous gifts of those like Barnabas in the church (see 4:34–35).[5]

Thus it's fair to say that Luke recognized in Dorcas a woman disciple who combined key attributes of ministry seen in the lives of Stephen and Barnabas. In addition, Acts 9:31 overviews the growing ministry of the church in the region that included Joppa as being in the power of the Holy Spirit. Thus even though Dorcas isn't directly said to be "full of the Holy Spirit," as are Stephen and Barnabas, that can be rightly assumed from the reference to the Spirit's role in 9:31.

Further, the wider evangelistic outcome of the ministries (and with Stephen and Dorcas, deaths) of all three is notably similar. This is seen by observing the growth summaries that appear in Acts in connection with each of them.

In between the descriptions of Stephen being "full of faith and of the Holy Spirit" (6:5) and "full of grace and power" (6:8), Luke summarizes, "And the word of God kept on spreading; and the number of the disciples continued to increase greatly in Jerusalem" (6:7). In a related passage we are told of the impact of "those who were scattered because of the persecution that arose in connection with

Stephen" on beyond Lydda, Joppa, and Caesarea, up the Mediterranean coast to Phoenicia, Cyprus, and Syrian Antioch (Acts 11:19). Through their evangelistic efforts, "a large number who believed turned to the Lord" (11:21). That leads next to the summary of the ministry of Barnabas in Antioch: "And considerable numbers were brought to the Lord" (11:24).

In other words, Stephen's Holy Spirit–empowered ministry produced growth in the church (6:5–7), as did his death (11:19–21). Likewise, Barnabas's generosity (4:36–37) and ministry (11:22–24) brought about real growth for God's people. Thus it is certainly not too much to conclude that Dorcas's similarly described generous ministry, death, and resurrected life should be understood as every bit as essential to the summary that "many believed in the Lord" (9:42) in Joppa as were Stephen's and Barnabas's roles in the church's ongoing expansion.

A Lifestyle of Good Works

In this flattering comparison of wording to Stephen and Barnabas another important aspect of Dorcas's life can be completely overlooked. That dimension is captured by the NIV, which says Dorcas "was *always* doing good and helping the poor" (v. 36, italics added). The NASB reflects this habitual aspect with the description, "abounding with deeds of kindness and charity, *which she continually did*" (v. 36, italics added).

Despite the differences in translation, both clearly indicate that Dorcas's good works and generosity to those in need were a lifestyle. That realization marks Dorcas as a model in regard to a wider, crucial consideration besides the spotlighted mention of her as a female disciple: the divinely intended lifestyle for all Christians.

Luke's mentor, the apostle Paul, emphatically denies that works have any place in becoming a Christian: "For by grace you have been saved through faith; and that not of yourselves, it is a gift of God; not as a result of works, that no one should boast" (Eph. 2:8–9). Yet, in completely ruling out good works in regard to initial salvation, he immediately clarifies that they are very important in regard to Christian living: "For we are His workmanship, created in Christ Jesus for good works, which God prepared beforehand, that we should walk in them" (Eph. 2:10). In essence, what Paul is saying here is, "Good works can't save you; only God's grace can. However, if you're grateful, your salvation will begin what God designed to be a lifestyle of good works." It also appears that Ephesians 2:10 is asserting that Christians most clearly evidence that they are a worthy creation, a "work of art"[6] of the Divine Artist, by an ongoing "walk" (i.e., lifestyle) of good works.

Nor is this the only passage in which Paul indicates that good works are at the heart of Christian living. In Titus 2:14, the apostle forcefully states that the redemption and purification of believers by Christ Jesus on the cross was to produce, literally, "zealots for good works." Then, a few verses later, he returns to a very similar theme to that expressed in Ephesians 2:8–10. Because of God's mercy and grace, apart from works, those who have believed in the incredible inheritance of eternal salvation through Christ should give constant heed to "engage in good works" (Titus 3:5–8).

Certainly Dorcas is a classic example of the obedience required in all three of these challenging passages. She is nothing less than a true masterpiece of God's re-creative artistry (Eph. 2:10) put on display by Luke in the narrative of Acts. By all indications of the appreciation of the other Christians in Joppa, she had distinguished herself as a loving zealot for good works (Titus 2:14) through the careful, ongoing pattern of her life.

Thus Dorcas is a beautiful, down-to-earth example of someone who was not a superspiritual celebrity but who lived a lifestyle of good works day after day in the real world. Based on Luke's short but sweet description of this woman's way of life, she would make both the discipleship and the godly works halls of fame.

This godly and consistent lifestyle definitely made Dorcas a valuable disciple in the church at Joppa. It also goes a long way toward explaining the rather amazing manner in which her fellow disciples responded to her death. Her passing undoubtedly left a huge hole in the church's wider ministry and, specifically, the ministry to widows in their midst (Acts 9:39).

Preparing the Body for . . . Resurrection

Because of the high esteem in which she was held in Joppa, Dorcas was honored in the way that her body was handled after her apparently sudden death (Acts 9:37). That honor, however, was hardly the normal preparation for burial. In fact it probably is not too much to say that the believers in Joppa had no intention of burying her body until they were convinced that God refused to miraculously resurrect her.[7]

Several things in the next few verses mark the description of Dorcas's death and its aftermath as of huge significance to Luke. For example, we find here the only mention of an actual death in Acts, as well as the only usage of *washed* (9:37) and *body* (9:40).

Second, the striking mention of Dorcas's dead body being laid "in an upper room" (9:37) immediately calls to mind the setting in which the apostles had prayed after the resurrection of Jesus (Acts 1:13–14), looking ahead to Pentecost. Perhaps that episode served as a strong encouragement to the disciples at Joppa after Dorcas died.

The third, and most unexpected, feature encountered here is the incomplete nature of the preparation of Dorcas's dead body. It appears that the other Christians in Joppa indeed began the process as would be expected by washing the body. Normally, however, they would immediately anoint the body and then wrap it with spices as had been done with the dead body of Jesus (John 19:39–40). There is absolutely no mention of this standard procedure in Acts 9.

In addition, "the warm climate dictated a speedy burial,"[8] which definitely did not occur in this case. If Dorcas died and her body was laid in the upper room on one day, then the messengers were dispatched by the church the next morning, it would have been sometime that next afternoon, at the earliest, when the messengers and Peter arrived back in Joppa.[9] Thus the risk of the beginning of a stench from the dead body was a very real, practical consideration (John 11:39).

In Jewish society, this kind of behavior went very much against accepted practice. "The value of proper interment in Jewish tradition"[10] was a considerable expectation in such a culture. So strong was the faith of the disciples at Joppa that Dorcas could be resurrected by Peter (Acts 9:38) that they were willing to run the risk of being severely criticized for denying Dorcas's body a decent burial in order to allow the opportunity for a glorious resurrection.

Rise to Walk in *Sameness* of Life

Many times at the conclusion of a baptism, the pastor will allude to the wording in Romans 6:3–4 by saying, "Rise to walk in newness of life!" That is meant as a challenge to break with old patterns of living in the resurrection power of Christ. The person being baptized has not died physically, of course, but is identifying fully with Jesus' death and resurrection (Col. 2:12).

In the case of Dorcas, she had died physically and had almost certainly been dead for at least a day. That is when Peter prayed and commanded, "Tabitha, arise" (Acts 9:40). She immediately was raised up and then was joyfully presented to the rest of the church (9:41).

It is believed by some that Peter's command and the ensuing miracle of Dorcas's resurrection is something of an echo of Jesus' raising of the synagogue official's daughter in Mark 5:35–42. It is true that "Talitha" (Mark 5:41) and "Tabitha" (Acts 9:40) are only a single letter different and that *arise* is the trigger word in both cases.[11]

Such an intended comparison would be clear if the resurrection of the synagogue official's daughter was found in Luke's first volume, the third Gospel, rather than in Mark. In Luke, however, there is a similar passage: the raising of the son of the widow of Nain (Luke 7:11–15). However, the wording of this Luke passage is not nearly as similar to Acts 9:40–41 as is Mark 5:41. On the other hand, the compassion that Jesus had for that widow and her comfort in receiving back from the dead her only son (Luke 7:12–13), almost certainly her lone means of support, does compare quite closely to Acts 9. Thus it is much more likely that Luke was thinking of Luke 7 when he penned Acts 9:36–43.

The Difference One Disciple Can Make

When Peter arrived in Joppa, he was immediately hurried to the upper room where Dorcas's body was laid (Acts 9:39). But surprisingly he was not given the immediate opportunity to raise Dorcas from the dead. He was first shown the fruit of Dorcas's labors by those who had been the primary recipients of her generosity, the widows.

Apparently the widows paraded by Peter and displayed for him "all the tunics and garments that Dorcas used to make while she was with them" (Acts 9:39). Though there probably were some garments laid out or being carried, it is quite likely that these widows were virtually all *wearing* clothes that Dorcas had made.[12]

It is impossible to know for sure why these widows chose to engage in a sort of ancient fashion show. Perhaps it was an appropriate part of their process of honoring the death of their dear friend and loving benefactor, Dorcas. It seems more likely, though, that the widows were doing their best to convince Peter that Dorcas was the kind of person and, more to the point, the kind of disciple who was worthy of being resurrected.

The widows were demonstrating how many lives of people with massive needs had been impacted for good on an ongoing basis by the single life of Dorcas. Her deeds of mercy included, among other things, keeping the necessary clothing on the backs of many widows who almost surely had no other means of support.

In Jerusalem there had been many generous people (Acts 4:34–37) as well as the special group of servants of the church that included Stephen (Acts 6:1–6) to provide for the Hellenistic widows. In Joppa, though, it was seemingly almost all on Dorcas's shoulders.

Dorcas had embodied what the apostle Paul meant by doing good "especially to those who are of the household of the faith" (Gal. 6:10). She undoubtedly had shown compassion toward other needy believers besides widows (Acts 9:36), but her ministry focus on widows, along with the earlier example of the church in Jerusalem (Acts 6:1–6), is very possibly a large part of the inspiration for the later detailed discussion of the support and conduct of widows in 1 Timothy 5:3–16. In that way, her example would help many other needy widows far beyond Joppa and the Jewish church over the centuries.

Whatever the extent of these comparisons, the points that must not be missed here are the *power* of the Lord in raising Dorcas and the compassionate *grace* displayed in bringing Dorcas back to minister to the widows. In her case, she would rise, literally, to the exact kind of lifestyle she had lived before: a continuation of her previous pattern of godly generosity.

Furthering the Great Commission

Besides the ecstasy of the church because of Dorcas's resurrection, there was a profound positive effect on the entire city of Joppa. As news of this amazing incident spread throughout the entire populace, the gospel message also spread like wildfire. As a result, "many believed in the Lord" (Acts 9:42).[13]

As noted earlier, this is a strategically placed growth summary that bridges between the regional summary in Acts 9:31 and the summary that speaks of the growing ethnic mix of the church in Syrian Antioch in Acts 11:20–21. Each of these summary statements is playing off Acts 1:8, Luke's statement of the Great Commission at the beginning of the book.

However, the description of Dorcas as a "female disciple" (9:36) and the church as "disciples" (9:38) also points to the Commission statement in Matthew 28:19–20. There the command of the risen Christ is to "make disciples," a process that must begin with evangelism (i.e., "Go" in v. 19). Since the only other place outside Matthew where this word translated "make disciples" (Greek *matheteuo*) is used is in Acts 14:21, it can be correctly assumed that Luke was familiar with the terminology in Matthew.[14]

So not only did Dorcas model the kind of discipleship that Jesus insisted on (Luke 14:26–35), she also provided the impetus for the rapid furthering of the initial witnessing step of the Great Commission through her death and resurrection (Matt. 28:19; Acts 1:8). No wonder Luke singled her out for special honor.

Why Not Dorcas?

At the beginning of this chapter, we addressed the question of why little-known Dorcas was chosen to be the only woman specifically called a disciple in the New Testament. That question has been more than answered: Dorcas's commitment and lifestyle clearly made her worthy to be a disciple of the Lord Jesus Christ.

So at this point the question is, "Why not Dorcas?" In other words, is there some preconceived notion that tends to prevent those reading Acts and those studying discipleship from appreciating how strongly Dorcas is featured by Luke? Does Luke's focus on Dorcas's unassuming and apparently lower-profile role cause discomfort for today's feminists? Or is it merely that she has gotten lost in the shuffle between the conversion of the apostle Paul in the earlier part of Acts 9 and the turning-point conversion of the Gentile, Cornelius, in Acts 10?

Ultimately, though, it is not as important why Dorcas has not received her just recognition as whether some semblance of scriptural balance can be brought about in the time ahead. Though Dorcas would have certainly never drawn attention to herself, her example of unselfish service is of great value for all disciples, especially in an era where recognition is often demanded and jealousy over prominent roles exists in many quarters.

Eight

PRISCILLA
Ready and Willing to Serve

Have you ever known an outgoing, articulate Christian woman who has an equally intelligent but quieter husband? Her strongest abilities may lie in the area of teaching, while his are in some other facet of Christian service. This kind of situation can sometimes give people the wrong impression. They think that because the wife is involved in a more visible ministry than her husband, she must be the more dominant one in the relationship.

They simply cannot picture this kind of woman in the role of a loving, submissive wife. Because the idea that an outgoing Christian wife could be joyfully submissive to a quieter, more reserved husband does not fit into their schema, such people draw wrong conclusions.

Now it is true that some outgoing (and some not so outgoing) Christian women do try to dominate their husbands and their homes. But the danger comes when we, without any concrete evidence, assume that a gregarious, charismatic woman would naturally be an unsubmissive wife.

From what the New Testament tells us of the prominent husband and wife team of Aquila and Priscilla, they could have been prime candidates for this kind of marital criticism. She was an intelligent, articulate woman, and he was an equally talented yet quieter man. But they worked together and complemented one another beautifully. As we study the life of Priscilla, we will discover just how biblically correct her marriage to Aquila was. As such, God greatly used this couple to bless and edify many in the early church. We will learn that Priscilla knew the delicate balance between *serving* side-by-side with her husband in the ministry and *submitting* to him in the home. She is a remarkable example of a willing and gifted disciple who served her husband and the early church with great fervor.

Kicked Out of Rome

Aquila, a native of Pontus (a region in Northern Asia Minor),[1] at some point made his home in Italy. It is not known for certain from where Priscilla originated, but it is quite possible that she was a native of Rome. Her formal name, Prisca (see Rom. 16:3; 1 Cor. 16:19; 2 Tim. 4:19), may lend support to this assumption. There is some evidence that she may have been connected with a prominent Roman family named Prisca.[2]

If so, Aquila and Priscilla probably met and married in Rome. While they were living there, the Emperor Claudius ordered that all Jews leave Rome (Acts 18:2). Apparently there was an uprising taking place among the Jews, which was causing significant problems in the entire city. Marshall explains, "This edict was associated with the Jews rioting *impulsore Chresto,* 'at the instigation of Chrestus' (according to Suetonius), a phrase which may well refer to trouble arising in the Jewish community as a result of the preaching of *Christus.*"[3] Footnoting the term *Christus,* Marshall goes on to talk about its significance: "The words *Chrestus* and *Christus* were pronounced in the same way, and Tacitus [first century Roman historian] referred to the Christians as *Chrestiani.*"[4] We do not know whether or not Aquila and Priscilla were part of this upheaval. But because of it, they likely heard the gospel and became Christians while they were at Rome.

It is a highly disturbing thing to be uprooted and kicked out of your home. In Aquila and Priscilla's case, though, it seems like it was providential. Had they not been ordered out of Rome at that time, they probably would have never gone to Corinth, which means they probably would never have met the apostle Paul.

Working with Paul

Aquila and Priscilla were already settled in Corinth when they met Paul (Acts 18:2). The text does not say exactly how they met, but it seems to indicate that their similar tentmaking[5] trade brought them together (Acts 18:3). Paul stayed and worked with Aquila and Priscilla while he "reasoned" with the Jews in the synagogue every Sabbath (Acts 18:4).

What is of particular interest to us here is that both Aquila *and* Priscilla were tentmakers. It appears that she was in business with her husband, which is no small thing. In fact, since she was quite likely associated with a prominent Roman family, Longenecker even suggests that "perhaps through Aquila's craftsmanship and Priscilla's money and contacts, they owned a tentmaking and leather-working firm."[6]

Hence, *together* they provided Paul with both Christian fellowship and a means to support himself. There is little doubt that both Aquila and Priscilla were also involved with Paul in his ministry there in Corinth. We do not know the level of their involvement with him in that region, but it's safe to assume that they were right there with him when he began to experience some opposition (Acts 18:6). The Lord appeared to Paul in a vision one night and encouraged him to stay in Corinth (Acts 18:9–10). So despite extreme hostility, Paul (and by implication, Aquila and Priscilla) stayed there for eighteen months, teaching the word of God (Acts 18:11). Aquila and Priscilla essentially worked behind the scenes, supporting Paul spiritually and emotionally. He desperately needed their support, because the widely accepted perversity and immorality of Corinth would have presented him with many challenges.

Crusade in Sin City

In his letter to the Romans, Paul wrote: "The law was added so that the trespass might increase. But where sin increased, grace increased all the more" (Rom. 5:20 NIV). The apostle must have pondered this truth when he entered Corinth. There he found a city permeated with blatant sin, but during his eighteen-month ministry there, the grace of God began to permeate the city through the preaching of the gospel.

Corinth was a very important city in the first century. Much like many of the large cities here in America, Corinth was immensely diverse in its people and culture. It was the capital of the province of Achaia and, because of its location, commerce, and abundant business opportunities, was one of the wealthiest metropolises in that region.[7]

Therefore, one of the many challenges Paul, Aquila, and Priscilla likely faced was that the people of this alluring city would have naturally been greatly distracted by worldly goods and pleasures. The overwhelming temptation to pursue fame and riches would have been in fierce competition with the things of the Spirit.

The Corinthian people were not completely without spiritual desire, however. The objects of their worship were scattered throughout their city. Religion was an intregal part of Corinthian life and perhaps posed the greatest challenge to Paul and his companions. These people probably grew up with their faith and were fairly set in their ways. Also, worship of their gods was often expressed through grotesque sexual immorality and perversity, capitalizing on natural human inclination. For this reason, these "sacred" practices attracted people from all over the known world. Mare describes how worship and other activities worked together to create this immoral atmosphere in Corinth:

> The celebration of the Isthmian games at the temple of Poseidon (Strabo 8.6.22) made a considerable contribution to Hellenic life. . . . But with the games there came an emphasis on luxury and profligacy, because the sanctuary of Poseidon was given over to the worship of the Corinthians' Aphrodite . . . whose temple on the Acrocorinth had more than 1,000 *hierodouloi* (female prostitutes). Strabo says (8.6.20) that many people came to Corinth on account of these priestesses, and the city grew rich. *Korinthiazomai* (meaning "to live like a Corinthian in the practice of sexual immorality") was the expression used at an earlier time . . . to describe a person of loose life.[8]

Paul, Aquila, and Priscilla had entered a virtual wasteland of morality. After eighteen months of ministry and of preaching and teaching the word of God (Acts 18:11), however, many Corinthians were transformed by the grace of God. It was a fruitful yet trying time of ministry for the three of them, and there can be no doubt their friendship grew. When the time came for Paul to move on, Aquila and Priscilla naturally accompanied him.

Moving the Ministry to Ephesus

By the time Aquila and Priscilla arrived at Ephesus (Acts 18:19), they had quite a bit of ministry experience. They most likely had been affiliated with the church at Rome before they were ordered to leave there, and they had just spent a year and a half serving with the apostle Paul in Corinth. This experience no doubt prepared them well for their future ministry, which was about to begin in Ephesus.

Aquila and Priscilla remained dear friends of Paul, but from this point on, the New Testament seems to indicate that they largely operated in ministry apart from him (See Rom. 16:3; 1 Cor. 16:19; 2 Tim. 4:19). They stayed in Ephesus while Paul sailed on to Syria (Acts 18:18–19). Ephesus was a major city in the province of Asia Minor, bustling with activities and full of opportunity for effective ministry.[9]

It is not known for certain how long Aquila and Priscilla stayed in Ephesus, but apparently they were there long enough to establish a fruitful ministry in their home (1 Cor. 16:19). Their time in Ephesus proved to be a turning point in their ministry relationship with the apostle Paul and with each other.

Reversing the Names but Not the Roles

A conspicuous and revealing literary phenomena takes place in Acts 18:18. Aquila's and Priscilla's names are suddenly reversed. This can hardly be an unintentional choice or mere happenstance. Luke seems to be purposefully communicating something very significant here about Priscilla and her role in ministry.

Priscilla "is more frequently named before her husband, which suggests that she was the more important figure from a Christian point of view."[10] Just how important Priscilla was will soon become more clear when we examine her encounter with Apollos. For now, it is crucial to point out that four out of the six times Priscilla and Aquila are mentioned, her name is indeed listed first (Acts 18:18–19, 26; Rom. 16:3; 2 Tim. 4:19).

However, the context of the two passages where Priscilla is *not* mentioned first gives us a fairly solid clue that their roles were not reversed. When the couple is initially introduced in Acts 18:2, Aquila is listed first. This was a typical order of introduction in Jewish circles and signified the male covering or authority. The other time Aquila is mentioned first is in 1 Corinthians 16:19, where the couple and the "church that meets at their house" (NIV) send greetings to the Corinthian church.

So in the context of introduction and in the context of the church meeting in their home, Aquila is listed first. The implication that can be drawn from these two passages is that, while Priscilla is the more important figure, Aquila's authority, both as a Christian leader and as the head of the home, is still very much recognized.

The point is that Priscilla was an educated, articulate disciple who came to the forefront of their ministry as a gifted teacher (see the following section). Yet she is still presented as one who recognized her husband's authority and willingly served side-by-side with him in the ministry. It does not seem that her insightful knowledge, as formidable as it apparently was, went to her head. Instead, she used her gifts in a biblically appropriate manner and was a benefit to many in the cause of Christ. The classic example of this is her interaction with Apollos.

Improving Apollos's Accuracy

Luke describes Apollos as a "learned man, with a thorough knowledge of the Scriptures. He had been instructed in the way of the Lord, and he spoke with great fervor and taught about Jesus accurately" (Acts 18:24–25 NIV). He was a native of Alexandria, where he was likely instructed in the Christian way, and he came to Ephesus to evangelize and possibly to seek further instruction.

Priscilla and Aquila first heard Apollos in the synagogue and "invited him to their home and explained to him the way of God more adequately" (Acts 18:26 NIV). Witherington eloquently points out Priscilla's role in the teaching session:

> We have a story about a husband and wife team of Christian missionaries and teachers. Luke's concern is not so much with what Apollos was taught by Priscilla and Aquila . . . or the results of that teaching, but that he was taught "more accurately" by this couple. . . .
> It is stated clearly that both she and Aquila instructed Apollos and her name is mentioned first, so that if anyone is indicated by Luke as the primary instructor, it is Priscilla. By "more accurately" Luke depicts Priscilla as expounding the matter further than basic Christian teaching, or at least in a way that involves the whole panorama of Christian teaching, so the place of the part would be seen in relation to the whole.[11]

This was indeed an intelligent and dynamic husband and wife team. If what Witherington has suggested is accurate, it seems that Priscilla led the way and made their ministry a more visible one. It is apparent that she took the initiative and invited Apollos into their home and together Priscilla and Aquila instructed him.

So this scene taken together with Paul's statement in 1 Corinthians 16:19 presents us with a beautiful portrait of a woman who was biblically balanced. She was not afraid to exercise her gifts but she also fully recognized her husband's giftedness and leadership. In this way, they beautifully complemented one another, and God was able to use them greatly.

This is a credit not only to Priscilla but also to Aquila, who appears not to have been threatened by his wife's extraordinary abilities. Instead, he set her free to use all the gifts God had given her. Had he not done this, it's possible that their ministry would have been seriously hindered, and we would have been lacking this remarkable portrait of an intelligent, capable disciple.

Paul's Admiration for Priscilla and Aquila

We have previously discussed the meeting and the subsequent close relationship that developed between Paul, Aquila, and Priscilla. We also noted that Aquila and Priscilla seem to have had a flourishing ministry quite separate from the apostle, while still remaining in close contact with him. Witherington notes: "Between Acts and Paul's letters we hear of them playing important roles in Ephesus, Corinth, and Rome. One gets the impression they were two of Paul's closest and most reliable workers, and it is likely they were involved in a wide range of activities from providing hospitality for Paul, to church planting, to teaching and preaching. . . . Clearly, they were a major factor in the Gentile mission."[12]

Paul's mention of Priscilla and Aquila in Romans 16:3–4 reveals his great admiration for them, not only for what they did for him, but also for the way they benefited many Gentile churches. The fact that they "risked their lives" (v. 4 NIV) for him is probably a reference to the riot that occurred in Ephesus because of the preaching of the gospel (Acts 19:28–31).

We know that the couple was in Ephesus at that time and that they had established a church in their home (Acts 18:19; 1 Cor. 16:8, 19). It is quite probable that Paul was staying with them, as he did in Corinth, and possibly even teaching the church that met in their home. "The disciples" mentioned in the context of the riot (Acts 19:30), who did not want Paul to appear before the crowd, could have been affiliated with him through Priscilla and Aquila's house church.

As Witherington pointed out through Paul's reference in Romans 16:4, the couple's ministry among the Gentiles was pervasive and fruitful. There is little doubt that they diligently taught the word of God, thus building up and edifying the church (Eph. 4:11–13).

However, what Paul did not mention about Priscilla and Aquila but is there by implication is their example of a well-balanced Christian marriage: he, a strong but quiet, gifted Christian leader, and she, an intelligent, articulate teacher. Two different personalities and two different roles, but together they represent a balanced, harmonious marriage relationship.

Harrison makes an insightful comment on Romans 16:3–4 concerning their marriage and, more specifically, concerning Priscilla's ministry role with her husband: "It has been observed that Priscilla and Aquila represent a splendid image of Christian married life. . . . Since several women are mentioned in this chapter, it is well to note that in addition to single women who served Christ, there was a married woman whom Paul encouraged to labor in the gospel along with her husband. Paul's habit of mentioning Priscilla first seems to testify to her great gifts and usefulness in the kingdom of God."[13]

A Very Gifted and Balanced Disciple

We have learned, then, that it is indeed possible to be an outgoing and gifted woman who is also a submissive and supportive wife. Priscilla is a marvelous example of a female disciple who knew the delicate balance between serving God's people through strong leadership skills and standing beside her husband as a supportive wife.

Priscilla is an incredible model of one who was ready and willing to serve. She was not afraid to exercise her spiritual gifts and, as a result, many (including her husband) were blessed and edified by her ministry. Here is a summary of her ministry and the gifts she exercised.

- Priscilla's ministry to Apollos (Acts 18:24–26): She brought him into her home and taught him the way of God more accurately. *The gifts of teaching and hospitality.*
- Priscilla's ministry to the apostle Paul (Rom. 16:3–4a): She risked her life for Paul. *The gift of mercy.*
- Priscilla's ministry to the Gentile churches (Rom. 16:4b): The Gentile churches were grateful for her help. *The gift of service/helps.*
- Priscilla's ministry in her home (1 Cor. 16:19): The church met in her home. *The gifts of service, hospitality, leadership, and teaching.*[14]

Priscilla teaches us that sometimes a gift is not really a gift until it is given away, especially when it comes to the work of the ministry. She shows us the value of being others-oriented, and in this way she will always be gratefully remembered.[15]

Nine

WOMEN IN ROME

Esteemed Servants of the Church

When it comes to building and maintaining a team perspective in almost any kind of organization, it's always wise to give credit where credit is due. That's especially true in a volunteer-oriented organization like the church of Jesus Christ, where most people are not receiving pay or the kinds of positive strokes they might get in the business world for their commitment and efforts.

Leaders do well to honor not only the achievements of those who work with them but also their good qualities. It makes a big difference to most people to know that those at higher levels of authority are aware of their accomplishments, strengths, or factors that helped bring about a task's successful conclusion or met a specific need.

In that light, the apostle Paul proves himself to be a very wise leader in Romans 16. The church at Rome was unique in its lack of relationship with Paul among all the churches to whom he wrote letters. The apostle had not been to Rome at this point and thus did not know the majority of the believers there.[1] Yet Paul bends over backward to give honor where it is due to those in Rome whom he knows are committed and deserving disciples, especially a sizable number of women.

Overcoming Distance

"Parting is such sweet sorrow" is a wonderful sentiment, but one that does not seem to have had a strong pull on Paul's personality. For example, in nine of his thirteen New Testament letters, his closing greetings[2] are little more than a (literary) wave of the hand. The four exceptions can be readily explained circumstantially (2 Timothy and Titus) and relationally (Romans and Colossians).

In 2 Timothy 4:9–21 most of the material is a concluding ministry update in light of the apostle's soon expected death (4:6–8, 18) with only a few greetings. Titus 3:12–15 speaks of arranging an important get-together with Titus in the time ahead, as well as the need to help coworkers along in their ministry. The greetings are only of the most general variety (v. 15).

With Colossians 4:7–18 and Romans 16:1–24 the greetings appear to reflect all the relational links Paul had with the believers in both locales, neither of which he had ministered in personally (Col. 2:1; Rom. 1:13–15). He hopes these personal contact points will positively represent both his ministry and his grasp of the situations in each church.[3]

In regard to Romans, it's not just a statistical oddity that of the forty uses of "greet/greetings" (Greek *aspazomai*) in Paul's letters, twenty-one are in Romans, all of which are in chapter 16.[4] Of those twenty-one, sixteen are extended by Paul (and his immediate coworkers) to members of the church in Rome, in stark contrast with only eight "to you" greetings and eleven "from me/us" greetings in his other epistles.

So what does this signify? The apostle decided to bridge the emotional separation of geographical distance and lack of face-to-face familiarity by drawing on every relational link he had in the church at Rome. In so doing, he demonstrated the same kind of personal-touch effectiveness of the ministry/missions prayer letter of recent years.

That is far from all that needs to be understood about the greeting section of Romans 16, however. It also proves to be the richest source of names (and often brief descriptions) of women disciples clustered in one passage in the entire New Testament.[5] Of the twenty-nine persons specifically named in Romans 16, at least nine are women:

Phoebe	vv. 1–2
Prisca (a.k.a. Priscilla)	vv. 3–4
Mary	v. 6
Tryphaena	v. 12
Tryphosa	v. 12
Persis	v. 12
Rufus's mother	v. 13
Julia	v. 15
Nereus's sister	v. 15
Junia (quite possibly)	v. 7[6]

Women Disciples Positioned for Honor

It is impressive that roughly one third of the disciples named in Romans 16 are women. But at least as amazing is the fact that three of the first five people whom Paul mentions in the chapter are women.

Anyone who grew up in the South prior to 1970 learned that "ladies first" was one of most basic tenets of Southern courtesy. Though many contemporary feminists either take exception to or get angry at what they perceive to be sexism in such a gesture, it need not mean anything more than politeness and respect. By contrast, the majority of women even today still very much appreciate the effort and sensitivity of men who step aside or open doors for them—at least they appreciate those who do not destroy their otherwise gentlemanly act with a lecherous stare or remark.

Certainly, in many different kinds of situations, going first should be considered a real honor. On the other hand, it must be admitted that saving the best for last can be just as much of an honor in other settings. In the case of Romans 16, however, it seems quite clear that the apostle Paul's inclusion of several women near the beginning of the passage is for the purpose of accolades.

Actually the placement of the glowing descriptions of Phoebe and Priscilla (16:1–4) serves two purposes here:

1. It focuses the initial attention of the apostle's concluding section on these two distinguished female disciples.
2. It also sensitizes the reader for the mentioning of the women disciples, which continues consistently through the greetings section (Rom. 16:1–16).

Phoebe: the Right Person for the Job

If it is a surprise that the Romans 16 greetings section begins with the mention of a woman (16:1–2), the surprises are just beginning. That woman, Phoebe, was not even a member of the church at Rome. Also, she was the only person of whom Paul says "I commend. . . ." Further, she is the only woman in the New Testament to whom the Greek term *diakonos* (which is elsewhere translated as "servant," "minister," and "deacon") is specifically applied.

If that was not enough, it is almost certain that Phoebe delivered Paul's letter to the Roman church.[7] This has spiritual significance because in carrying the letter for the apostle, Phoebe was acting as his representative to the church at Rome, even if her primary reason for going to Rome was some other type of business.[8] That is a key role Paul normally reserved for a trusted coworker like Tychicus (Eph. 6:21–22; Col. 4:7–8) or someone who already had a close relationship to the church in question, like Epaphroditus (Phil. 2:25–29).

Because the apostle's name and the well-being of the church were on the line, the person presenting the letter also acted as a representative of the gospel through his or her personal words and works. As will be seen, even if no other woman in the New Testament is seen playing such a role, Phoebe clearly is the right disciple for the job.

Because Phoebe was such an exemplary person, the apostle wanted two things to take place:

1. He wanted her to be properly appreciated because of what she had done in the past.
2. He wanted her to be appropriately treated on her arrival in Rome as well as receive whatever help she might need.

These twin concerns stand out clearly in Romans 16:1–2. Paul begins and ends by emphasizing the kind of ministry by which Phoebe had already distinguished herself in her home church: She was a significant "servant of the church" in Cenchrea (v. 1) and a generous "helper of many," including Paul (v. 2). In the middle, Paul directs the church at Rome as to the kind of ministry he wants them to have toward Phoebe: Receive her in a worthy, Christian manner, and help her in whatever she needs (v. 2).

A Leader Whether "Servant" or "Deaconess"

Perhaps the greatest ongoing misconception about leadership in the church of Jesus Christ is that it is primarily about position, title, and power. How quickly it is forgotten that the Lord Jesus himself spoke forcefully to that issue at the conclusion of the Last Supper in Luke 22:24–27. In response to the egotistical dispute about which disciple was the greatest, Jesus starkly contrasted the worldly outlook on greatness as power and authority with the servant-leadership that should characterize his disciples. Christ leaves no doubt that a true leader, from the perspective of his kingdom, is first and foremost a "servant" (Greek *diakonos;* vv. 26–27).

It is, of course, true enough that the term *diakonos* also quickly came to be used as both a general description for those who minister for the Lord (e.g., 1 Cor. 3:5; 1 Thess. 3:2) and a title for a local church office (Phil. 1:1; 1 Tim. 3:8, 12).[9] Still, such usage does not erase the element of servanthood. If anything, it strengthens it because of the normal tendency of those living in this world to want to "lord it over" others as leaders (Luke 22:25).

Thus it can be readily seen that the ongoing debate over whether Phoebe was a *deaconess* of her church in Cenchrea or merely a *servant* of those in that congregation (Rom. 16:1) is imbalanced if not totally misguided. Ultimately, in the eyes of the Lord Jesus, Phoebe's reputation as a true *diakonos* of the church meant that she embodied Christ's prescribed demeanor for a disciple-leader (Luke 22:26).

It does seem slightly more likely that Phoebe may have been a "deaconness" (1 Tim. 3:10–11) because of Paul's strong commendation and sense of confidence in her ability to carry out her responsibility (Rom. 16:1).[10] But the real point here is that she was, by Jesus' standards, a truly great servant-leader and a disciple either way.

Roll Out the Welcome Mat

By the time Paul got around to commending Phoebe in Romans 16:1, he had already spoken to the Roman believers of the responsibilities of "contributing to the needs of the saints" and "practicing hospitality" (Rom. 12:13). With those words, it seems as if the wise veteran apostle was setting up the Roman congregation for their dealings with Phoebe. Even if that was not the case, however, Phoebe's arrival offered an immediate opportunity to apply both of Paul's admonitions.

Clearly, Phoebe was the kind of disciple who was worthy of honor (16:2), another of Paul's earlier behavioral guidelines in Romans 12:10. Since the church in Rome surely would have desired to properly host the apostle's representative, all that was needed from Paul had been done: his commendation (16:1) and his request for honored treatment (16:2).

Rolling out the red carpet spiritually may only overlap slightly with the way the world does things. With "the saints" (16:2), it is less the food, surroundings, or dress than the fellowship, appreciation, and genuine concern that is expressed. This kind of treatment would make this special disciple feel like "Saint Phoebe" both in Rome and in returning home to Cenchrea.

Helping the Helper

It is clear from Paul's words that Phoebe was a habitual helper (Rom. 16:2) back home in Cenchrea, but the nature of the help she provided is not as clear. The word translated "helper" (Greek *prostatis*) is not used elsewhere in the New Testament but was employed in Roman society to speak of a "legal representative," and in Jewish circles it could mean a wealthy "patron."[11]

Since the term is surely used figuratively in verse 2, it could speak of help related to advocacy for the needy and afflicted, somewhat like Dorcas in Acts 9. It could, of course, also refer to outright generous personal giving, much like Lydia in Acts 16. Even if Phoebe was well-to-do, however, her bankroll was not unlimited. Though there is no way to discern what was involved, she would need assistance while in Rome (Rom. 16:2) and, most likely, on her return trip to Cenchrea.

This meant that many of the disciples in the church at Rome had the opportunity and blessing to help one who had long since made her name as a helper. It also meant that Phoebe came to understand just how refreshing the kind of help she had rendered to so many, including Paul (16:2), truly was.

Hardworking Disciples

If Romans 16 begins as if it is meant to be a special commendation for Phoebe (16:1–2) and a heartfelt decoration for bravery for Prisca (and Aquila, her husband; 16:3–4), the descriptions of the other female disciples have to rank as substantial honorable mentions. In fact the compact descriptions of four of these women indicate that they compare favorably to Phoebe and Prisca in the intensity of their commitment to the Lord and his people.

An otherwise unknown Mary (16:6),[12] Tryphaena, Tryphosa, and Persis (16:12) are all called "hard workers" by Paul. In each case, the Greek term is *kopiao*, which means to do work that makes you tired or weary.[13] Since Paul knew well what it was like to work hard in ministry (Col. 1:29; 1 Tim. 4:10; 2 Tim. 2:6), he greatly appreciated that attribute.

This is not to say that Paul was seeking workaholic disciples. It is altogether too easy to get so preoccupied with laboring for the Lord that you overlook walking with the Lord, the vertical dimension of being a disciple. Still, if elders "who work hard at preaching and teaching" (1 Tim. 5:17) are worthy of double honor, others who work in the Lord's service should certainly receive honor. Paul's greetings to these four women disciples seem to reflect such an understanding.

Outstanding among the Apostles

If the Junias in Romans 16:7 is a woman (Junia), she is probably the wife of Andronicus.[14] Although Paul calls them his "kinsmen" (NASB) or "relatives" (NIV), there is no way to finally determine whether they were Paul's blood relatives, though their earlier salvation (i.e., "in Christ before me," 16:7) would seem to argue against that, since there is no other clear evidence of believers in Paul's family. Even if they were simply dear Christian brethren, their relationship with the apostle still had deep roots. They apparently had either endured jail time together at some point or lived through some very similar circumstances related to imprisonment in the cause of Christ.[15] Experiencing such common ordeals certainly makes you feel a close kindred bond.

Further, the reputation of these coworkers of Paul—whether husband and wife or two men does not alter the point—was that they are "outstanding among the apostles" (16:7). This can mean that the pair had a splendid long-term track record in the eyes of the apostles like Paul, Peter, and John, and that would be impressive enough. However, broader uses of the idea of "apostle" in Paul's letters, like those that include Silas and Timothy (1 Thess. 1:1; 2:6) or Epaphroditus (Phil. 2:25), would seem to indicate that this dynamic duo of disciples would be viewed today as highly honored veteran missionaries, those "sent out" (Greek *apos-*

tello) by the church for pioneering ministry.[16] If such an understanding is correct, they were taking very seriously the need to go to the end of the earth (Acts 1:8), and in the process, they beat Paul to Rome.

Three More for Good Balance

When it looks like something has been added near the end, it is often said to be there "for good measure." Certainly it would be neat and tidy if the apostle simply threw in the names of three more women disciples to get to the nice round number of ten (if "Junia" is understood instead of "Junias"). However, if Paul has a discernible motive in including Rufus's mother (Rom. 16:13), Julia, and Nereus's sister (16:15), it would seem more likely that their names represent *spiritual balance.*

Earlier in the chapter, Paul had greeted and described some high-profile (or at least highly productive) female disciples. Certainly Phoebe (vv. 1–2) and Priscilla (vv. 3–4) would be considered hard acts to follow. Perhaps even the references to Mary (v. 6), Tryphaena, Tryphosa, and Persis (v. 12) are intimidating to less assertive readers.

Now, though, things get balanced out. Other than the implied motherly affection and understanding, nothing whatsoever is said about the achievements of Rufus's mother as a disciple. Even less is said about Julia and Nereus's sister. Yet they are still special to Paul, even though they seem to be ordinary disciples of the Lord going about their lives in a tranquil, quiet, godly, and dignified manner (1 Tim. 2:1–2).

There is the balance that is so often overlooked. It is not necessary to be a *splashy* disciple to be a *special* disciple. It is obviously not as noticeable to other people when a disciple is serving behind the scenes, but it is equally noteworthy before the Lord. Nor does age matter: Rufus's mother was almost certainly older, while Nereus's sister was likely a good bit younger than Paul.

If you are quiet or shy, when you get to heaven you might want to take the opportunity to look up Rufus's mother, Julia, and Nereus's sister. After all, they are examples of unassuming disciples whom the great, energetic, dynamic apostle Paul refused to overlook. He needed them for good balance, and so does the church at the end of the twentieth century.

Discipleship and Spiritual Warfare

The Romans 16 greetings section apparently ends with Paul admonishing his readers to "greet one another with a holy kiss" (16:16). Then, at first glance, it seems that the apostle disconnectedly launches into dealing with people attempting to cause dissension in the church at Rome (16:17–19). Finally, he mentions the inevitable defeat of Satan (16:20a), before turning to a benediction and further greetings (16:20b–23).

This section actually has a more direct purpose than it initially appears. Since it was an *unholy* kiss that was the vehicle by which Judas betrayed Jesus (Luke 22:47–48), the possibility of spoiling the unity among the disciples (Rom. 16:17–19) by a kiss with questionable motives is considerable. The potential difficulty is increased greatly when it is members of the opposite gender who are kissing.

The admonition to a "holy kiss" must be read carefully. A disciple, whether male or female, cannot be too careful. For example, even though Paul had already told Timothy to be exemplary in his moral purity (1 Tim. 4:12), he comes back less than half a chapter later to reiterate that Timothy, apparently a bachelor, needed to be extremely careful to treat "the younger women as sisters, in all purity" (1 Tim. 5:2).

What was intended to be an avenue of mutual *spiritual* edification can be subtly changed into an exercise in sneaky *sensual* gratification. Thus, the appropriate level of caution always demands that the disciple be "wise in what is good, and innocent in what is evil" (Rom. 16:19).[17] There is no easier way for a disciple to destroy his or her testimony than by moral impurity. Satan particularly enjoys such moral self-destruction among the Lord's servants, and he is the one who stands to gain the most.

On the other hand, if the unity among the disciples in the church remains strong and pure, wise and innocent (16:17–19), Satan is in the process of going down to defeat (16:20), even long before his eternal torment in the lake of fire (Rev. 20:10). As Romans 16 strongly implies, it is the commitment, courage, hard work, and pure brother-sister relationships in the church that set Satan up to be finally crushed, as Genesis 3:15 originally predicted.[18]

Paul understood that well. He was doing his utmost to protect the disciples in Rome from the lurking dangers of discouragement, envy, sensuality, and disunity. Will disciples in our day, female and male alike, take to heart the two-pronged message of Romans 16? It is a call to be honorable and hardworking and a caution to be wise as a serpent and innocent as a dove.

Ten

WOMEN IN PHILIPPI
Partners in the Gospel

If discipleship were a business, some people might mistakenly view it as a sole proprietorship. The reason for this is that there has been an imbalanced focus on the individual disciple by some writing for and working in discipleship ministries. Certainly the individual is very important and should never be underemphasized. However, the Book of Acts in general and the founding of the church at Philippi in particular make it clear that such individual disciples play a larger role as the building blocks of the corporate church.

This means that discipleship is at least as much a partnership as it is individual proprietorship. It also means, as with any partnership, that there will be the ongoing challenge of keeping unity among the partners.

In recent years some valuable specialized studies on the women in the Philippian church have appeared.[1] Each of these has concluded in one way or another that the female believers spotlighted in the Epistle to the Philippians and Acts 16—where the church at Philippi is founded—played quite prominent roles in the overall development of that congregation. It also should be remembered that Philippi is the only church the apostle Paul commended for "your partnership in the gospel from the first day until now" (Phil. 1:5 NIV).[2]

Evidence of the Women Disciples' Prominence in Philippi

In almost any criminal court case, there will be legal maneuvering over pieces of evidence that could potentially be decisive in proving the defendant's innocence or guilt. Of course, most cases are not decided on the basis of one piece of evidence alone but rather by an interconnected pattern of the evidence.

Women in Acts 16

There are seven lines of evidence in Acts 16 that demonstrate the prominence of certain women in that congregation. Each individual point is significant, but taken together the following factors create a very strong pattern:

1. *The church at Philippi is the only church founded in Acts in which two individual women are spotlighted.* Table 9 shows that only the church in Jerusalem received two of Luke's focus points on women—one of which was negative (Sapphira) and the other general (the Greek-speaking widows). Priscilla is mentioned twice but as Paul's mobile coworker in Corinth (Acts 18:2–3) and Ephesus (Acts 18:18–19).

Thus the conversions of Lydia and the woman freed from demonic possession (16:14–18), modest though the mentions may seem at first glance, stand out in the narrative of Acts. That parallels the spotlight on Euodia and Syntyche in Philippians.

Table 9
Focal Women in Churches Started in the Book of Acts

Churches	Jerusalem	Samaria	Syrian Antioch	Asia Minor	*Philippi	Thessalonica	Berea	Athens	Corinth	Ephesus
Passage in Acts	Chapters 2–7	Chapter 8	Chapters 5, 11, 13	Chapters 13–14	Chapter 16	Chapter 17	Chapter 17	Chapter 17	Chapter 18	Chapters 18–20
Women Spotlighted	Sapphira (negatively) Hellenistic widows (corporately)	None	None	None	Lydia (formerly) demon-possessed woman	Leading women (generally)	Leading women (generally)	Damaris (mention only)	Priscilla	Priscilla
Time Spent There	Several years	Weeks or months	Approaching 2 years	Several months	Several months	About a month	Weeks	Weeks or months	Over one and a half years	Well over 2 years

2. *These two women in Acts 16 are the first women singled out for development as characters on Paul's missionary journeys.*[3] Of the two, Lydia is the first recorded convert as the missionaries led by Paul move onto the European continent (16:11–15). If nothing else, her conversion is a major milestone in the Christian witness as it progresses to the ends of the earth (Acts 1:8).

3. *The strong wording "the Lord opened her heart" (16:14) reflects importance in God's eyes as he intervenes to convert the foundational person in Philippi: Lydia.* Even if the conversion of many of the brothers and sisters in the church at Philippi (16:40) can't be tied in a direct scriptural sense to Lydia's conversion, her faith almost certainly had an influential domino effect in her household (16:15) and within the women's prayer meeting (16:13, 16).[4]

4. *Lydia and the woman released from demons are two of the three founders seen in the unfolding story of the beginning of the Philippian church (Acts 16:12–40).* Further, since the Philippian jailer, the third founder, does not come to faith until sometime later (16:30–34), their foundational role is even more evident in this passage.[5]

5. *Because Lydia was a successful businesswoman (16:14), she had a large enough house to take in Paul's missionary band (16:15) and to provide a meeting place for the church (16:40).* Those factors would have automatically made Lydia a central part of the earlier stages of the development of the Philippian church.

6. *Since the author's perspective changes from "they" (third person) to "we" (first person) in Acts 16:10, it's strongly implied that Luke was an eyewitness to the roles of Lydia and the demonized slave girl.*[6] If this is correct, Luke was personally very impressed with the crucial role of women in the emerging church in the strategic city of Philippi.

7. *As has been seen before, the wording "a certain . . ." before the naming of Lydia (Acts 16:14) is a means of emphasis.*[7] Fur-

ther, the wording "a certain woman named . . ." is the counterpart to the earlier description of Cornelius (Acts 10:1). That is important because, as Cornelius was the first emphasized Gentile convert, Lydia is the first emphasized convert in Europe. Also, it is probably to be understood as parallel to the wording "a certain disciple," which introduces key characters like Ananias of Syrian Antioch (9:10) and Timothy (16:1). Most tantalizing of all, however, is the comparison with "a certain female disciple named Tabitha" (9:36). The striking similarity implies that Lydia is being introduced as a very important female disciple "waiting to happen," following after the pattern of Tabitha/Dorcas.

Women in the Philippian Letter

There are also seven angles from which the foundational significance of some of the women involved in the planting of the church at Philippi is seen in the Philippian letter. Again, each point carries considerable weight, but the combined case is overwhelming.

1. *Philippians is the only letter Paul wrote in which two women in the church being addressed are emphasized in the body of the Epistle.*[8] As can be seen in table 10, Phoebe and Priscilla are both discussed briefly in Romans 16 as are Eunice and Lois in 2 Timothy. However, Phoebe is not a member of the church in Rome (Rom. 16:1), and Priscilla had traveled in ministry with Paul (Acts 18–19) until shortly before the writing of Romans. Also, Lois and Eunice (2 Tim. 1:5) were not members of the church at Ephesus and were almost certainly not present there when 2 Timothy was received.

2. *Euodia and Syntyche (Phil. 4:2) are the only other members of the Philippian church who are clearly named, beside Epaphroditus (2:25; 4:18) and Clement (4:3).* The simple proportion of two out of four church members named certainly emphasizes the women, Euodia and Syntyche. That is espe-

Table 10
Focal Women in Churches Addressed in Paul's Letters

Churches	Rome	Corinth	Galatia	Ephesus	Philippi	Colossae	Thessalonica	Crete
Related Letter(s)	Romans	1, 2 Corinthians	Galatians	Ephesians, 1, 2 Timothy	Philippians	Colossians, Philemon	1, 2 Thessalonians	Titus
Women Spotlighted in the Letters	Phoebe (from Cenchrea) Prisca (known from Corinth and Ephesus)	Chloe (in passing) Prisca (in Ephesus)	None	Eunice Lois (in Asia Minor)	Euodia Syntyche (Only epistle that names two women native to that church and in significant roles)	Apphia	None	None

cially true since Epaphroditus is apparently carrying the letter from Paul (Phil. 2:25), and Clement is mentioned only alongside the women in 4:3, as *another* esteemed fellow worker.

3. *The description "who have shared my struggle in the cause of the gospel" (Phil. 4:3) indicates that Euodia and Syntyche had previously been models of the kind of behavior Paul was now urging for the Philippian congregation (1:27).* That point is even stronger when it is realized that "striving together" (Greek *sunathleo*) is found in the New Testament only in Philippians 1:27 and 4:3.

4. *The verses focusing on Euodia and Syntyche (4:2–3) are parallel to the earlier challenge to unity (2:2–4) in the overall inverted structuring of Philippians.*[9] This indicates they are the key to the disunity that had begun to trouble that church. Table 11 clearly visualizes that Philippians 1:27–2:4 and 4:1–5 are the third (C) layer of the overarching inverted structure of Philippians.[10]

5. *The repeated use of urge in regard to both Euodia and Syntyche (Phil. 4:2) reflects an individualized sense of prominence in Paul's eyes.* On that point, Peter O'Brien astutely comments: "This heightens the effect, as Paul refuses to take sides but makes the same appeal to both. It is as if . . . he is exhorting each separately face to face."[11] O'Brien goes on to say that if these two women were not very important in regard to the church's present circumstances, "it is difficult to explain why their names were mentioned in a letter to be read publicly in church."[12]

6. *Counting these women along with "the rest of my fellow workers" (Phil. 4:3) shows their prominence in regard to the wider ministry that Paul had begun in Philippi.* That point is underlined when it is realized that the only other usage of "fellow worker" in Philippians refers to Epaphroditus (2:25), whom Paul strongly commends as worthy of honor by the church at Philippi (2:29).

Table 11

Inverted Structure of Philippians

(1:1–2) Opening Greetings: Previewing partnership theme; emphasizing servant-leadership

  A. (1:3–11) Prologue: "Partnership in the gospel" theme introduced with prayerful gratitude

    B. (1:12–26) Comfort/Example: Paul's safety and right thinking in the midst of a difficult "guarded" situation

      C. (1:27–2:4) Challenge: Stand fast and be united, fulfilling Paul's joy

        D. (2:5–16) Example/Action: Christ's example of humility and suffering before glory, then related behavioral instructions

          E. (2:17–3:1a) Midpoint: Caring models of gospel partnership, two of which are sent to help immediately

        D'. (3:1b–21) Example/Action: (Paul's example of humbling and suffering before upward call/transformation, then instructions

      C'. (4:1–5) Challenge: Stand fast and accentuate existing joy by the reconciliation of two past gospel partners

    B'. (4:6–9) Comfort/Example: The Philippians' "guarded" peace of mind and right thinking in the midst of an anxious situation

  A'. (4:10–20) Epilogue: Partnership from the past renewed with expressed gratitude

(4:21–23) Closing Greetings: Reviewing partnership theme, emphasizing oneness of the saints

7. Paul makes a pun on the names of both Euodia and Syntyche to enhance his practical application for the entire church. The name Euodia sounds to the ear exactly like the Greek word *euodia* ("good smell"), which is found in Philippians 4:18,[13] and it should be remembered that the letter would have been initially read out loud in the church. That unavoidable similarity ironically implies that Euodia should live up to her name and be a pleasant aroma before the Lord.

Also, Syntyche includes the Greek prefix *sun-*, which means "together with." In Philippians there are fifteen *sun-* prefix terms, indicating a pattern of usage related to partnership and unity.[14] That this is also a challenge for Syntyche to live up to her name is very likely because of the clustering of this *sun-* terminology in 4:3.[15]

All this evidence shows the prominence of Euodia and Syntyche in regard to the past and present of the church at Philippi. Factors ranging from overall structure to subtle puns all underline their prominent roles in both the joyful and not so happy times of that growing congregation. If anything, their present problem-causing status (4:2–3) and the parallelism by which the apostle calls attention to it (2:2–4, then 4:2–3) only indicates just how important these two women were to the Philippian church at the time Paul addressed them.

Lessons for Modern Disciples

The women focused on in Acts 16 and the Philippians letter are seen as prominent in the church at Philippi. In fact, it is not too much to say that the author's portrayal presents those women as absolutely essential to the foundational development of that congregation that Paul loved "with the affection of Christ Jesus" (Phil. 1:8 NIV). But what else can we learn from these women disciples as individuals and from their individual situations?

Hosting Missionaries and the Church

What kind of woman would head off to a regular Saturday prayer meeting and return home with a group of previously unknown missionaries who were going to stay in her home indefinitely? Either a very naive woman or a very generous one.

In this case, it was certainly not a case of naivete. Lydia was an astute and successful businesswoman (Acts 16:14). As such, she could afford to be generous. And she certainly was to Paul, Silas, Timothy, and Luke, the recently arrived missionaries.

Lydia's generosity in asking Paul and the others to become houseguests and use her home as their base of operations in Philippi was largely due to her overwhelming sense of gratitude. The Lord had enabled her to respond to the message that Paul had shared with all the ladies present at the Sabbath prayer meeting (16:13–14). She had already been a worshiper of the one true God, and now that more general faith had been clarified and completed.

Besides her own personal conversion, Lydia had the responsibility of other family members (neither husband nor children are specifically mentioned) and servants who made up her "household" (16:15). Since she cared deeply about those people, she was very concerned to have them immediately exposed to the gospel. As Paul and the others proclaimed that life-giving message, the response was apparently unanimously positive, culminating in a family baptism service (v. 15).

It was at that point that Lydia prevailed upon Paul and his missionary coworkers to more or less take up residence temporarily in her home. Her normally prosperous occupation and her invitation to at least four persons indicates that she had a spacious dwelling. Further, the fact that all "the brethren" in Christ in Philippi were able to come together in Lydia's home after Paul and Silas were released from jail (16:35–40), implies that her house was very large indeed.

Given her well-to-do status, Lydia likely also played a key role in the past and recent financial gifts that Paul thanks the Philippian church for in Philippians 4:10, 14–18. Even though there almost certainly were other wealthy people in the church at Philippi, Lydia has a special place as the first spotlighted conversion in the city.

Also, in comparing Lydia's generosity to that of women disciples in the rest of the New Testament, she remains a standout. She joins the exclusive ranks of Martha of Bethany (Luke 10:38); Mary, John Mark's mother, in Jerusalem (Acts 12:12); Priscilla, in Rome and Corinth (Rom. 16:3–5; 1 Cor. 16:19); and Apphia, in Colossae (Philem. 2), all of whom opened their homes in the cause of the gospel. Certainly in Philippi, the initial foothold of Paul's ministry in Europe (Acts 16:9–14), Lydia was a very important hostess and benefactor.[16]

Release and Upheaval

On too many occasions, the evangelical church has been guilty of sensationalism. When a prominent entertainer, sports figure, or the like becomes a Christian, it is not uncommon that the spiritually newborn believer is put up front in order to get publicity and draw crowds.

The other situation that cranks up the sensationalism is when someone is converted out of the kind of shocking background that grips the interest of the masses. That has happened repeatedly with those who have come out of the dark underworlds of the drug culture and involvement in the occult or demonic realms.

The second woman introduced in Acts 16 is seen against just such a potentially sensationalistic backdrop: demon possession. Yet neither Paul nor Luke give in to the temptation to make a splash in telling of the spiritual freeing (and assumed conversion) of the unnamed slave-girl (Acts 16:16–18). They focus on what needed to be done but give no titillating information whatsoever.

The only two apparent reasons why the incident with the slave-girl is even brought up are:

1. The slave-girl provides a direct contrast with Lydia, the God-fearing businesswoman.
2. It leads into the reason why Paul and Silas are thrown in jail, where they meet the third key figure in Philippi—the jailer (16:19–23).

There is also a most intriguing angle on the casting out of the spirit inhabiting the slave-girl that has to do with the nature of discipleship. The demon in the girl obviously had her spiritually enslaved. Likewise, the girl's masters were making all the profit from her spirit of divination because she was their legal property as a slave (16:16–19). Ironically, the demon that controlled the girl's utterances not only recognized that Paul and the others were proclaiming "the way of salvation" (v. 17), which would result in the demon having to leave the girl, but it also clearly understood that Paul and the other missionaries were slaves in an even more profound way than the girl. Calling them "bond-servants" (Greek *douloi*, 16:17), meaning those who have *voluntarily* attached themselves to a master for willing service, shows an understanding of the commitment that Jesus asks of those who would follow him as disciples (Luke 14:26–33).

This also would likely have made the transition from being a demon-possessed slave to being a disciple of the Lord Jesus much more natural.[17] Since she well understood what was involved in service for a master, it would have been a joy and privilege for her to personally choose to serve the ultimately generous and loving Master of the entire universe.

What a great lesson this also is for modern disciples. It is infinitely preferable to be a *willing* bond-servant to the Lord than to be enslaved to any number of other relationships, addictions, or destructive influences.

When Partnership Becomes Conflict

It is always very sad to watch long-time, close friends become enemies. Such a tragic breakdown was causing a spiritual cancer to begin to grow at the heart of the Philippian church. At first glance it seems that Paul is trying to tiptoe lightly around this problem, which had been developing for some time, by vaguely appealing for unity and humility in the congregation (Phil. 2:2–4). But he chooses to name names in 4:2–3, putting his longstanding friendship/partnership with Euodia and Syntyche on the line.[18] The apostle handles things as sensitively and judiciously as possible. He is not overly critical. In fact, he goes out of his way to underline how much he and the Philippian church have profited from the willingness of these two women disciples to be involved as coworkers in the struggle to further the cause of the gospel (4:3). He also reiterates that, in spite of their current attitudes and actions, their "names are in the book of life" (4:3).

Paul also carefully avoids taking sides in any sense. He asserts that both are equally at fault, and painstakingly appeals to both (note the echoed "I urge") to "live in harmony in the Lord" (4:2). The repeated mention of "joy" (4:1) and "rejoice" (4:4) also strongly implies that Paul's joy in regard to the Philippian church would be the healing of the breach between these two influential women disciples (2:2).

The tone of 2:2–4 and 4:2–3 sounds as if both women were still active in the congregation, and both were probably present when Paul's letter was read to the congregation at large. It must have been quite a shock. But the truth of the matter was that if Euodia and Syntyche could each swallow her pride (2:3–4), make peace, and work together as before, it would be a tremendous reason for the whole church to rejoice (4:4).

It is frustrating to some readers to realize that there is absolutely no clue as to how this dispute began or what it was about. However, that may well be for the best. Such arguments, whether open, the silent treatment, or behind the other person's back, happen for reasons ranging from minor misunderstandings to things that are truly crucial. Determining who is right in such an issue soon becomes secondary to the need to deal with the angry, sinful underlying attitudes, because such disputes offer Satan a foothold in your individual and corporate life (Eph. 4:26–27). That is an incredibly high price to pay for winning an argument.

May the shadows of Euodia and Syntyche hang long over disciples today. On the one hand, there is much to be learned from their ongoing gospel partnership roles that is very positive (Phil. 1:3–5). On the other hand, it is all too easy to let self-centered pride (2:3–4) create a wall between those who have walked together in following Christ (4:2–3). In other words, we should emulate their good example but avoid the kind of stubborn dispute that was rapidly making their church a war zone.

The Dark Side of Prominence

Unfortunately, it is not known from the New Testament or history whether Euodia and Syntyche resolved their conflict and again became exemplary partners in the gospel (Phil. 1:5, 27). Still, with Fred Craddock, "We can hope Euodia and Syntyche were mature enough to accept" the admonition of Paul and the help of other concerned believers.[19] All things considered, it's not improbable that "Paul's plea was heeded."[20]

Whatever happened, though, the short-term behavior of the apostle's long-term female coworkers (4:3) in no way undercuts their prominence. Rather, it communicates a sobering note of reality that reminds readers today that even those who have distinguished themselves in the cause of the gospel can still get mired in disputes that, regardless of gender, potentially polarize an otherwise healthy congregation.

The practical bottom line here is that prominent roles among God's people require modeling the kind of Christ-like attitude (Phil. 2:5–11) and servant-leadership actions (Matt. 20:26–27) that make for the edification, unity (Phil. 2:2–4), and growing maturity (Eph. 4:11–13) of all believers in the church. For the most part, the spotlighted female disciples in the church at Philippi are excellent examples.[21]

Eleven

EUNICE

Discipleship in a Mixed Marriage

The author's extensive experience in Christian ministry has indicated that mixed marriages are quite common, even in evangelical churches. From a spiritual standpoint, a mixed marriage is a marital union in which one partner is a believer in Jesus Christ and the other is not.

Most spiritually mixed marriages in our society come about for one of three reasons:

1. A Christian falls in love with an unbeliever and knows it is wrong to marry him or her (2 Cor. 6:14–15)[1] but believes that their mutual love will, sooner or later, draw the other partner to saving faith in Jesus.

2. An immature Christian may be unaware of the danger
   of a lack of eternal spiritual compatibility (in Christ)
   and marry an unsaved person out of ignorance.
3. Two non-Christians marry, and one becomes a believer at some later point in their marriage.

It seems that there are more Christian women than men
in such mixed marriages. From my experience in premari-
tal and marriage counseling situations, it is more commonly
a self-deluded woman, whose spiritual relationship with
the Lord has been temporarily put on hold, who gets into
such a marriage. And, more often, it is the female partner
who comes to salvation midcourse in the marriage rather
than (or before) the man.

So the necessity of many Christian women having to
carve out their discipleship against the backdrop of such a
mixed marriage is a difficult reality. Thus it would be a
tremendous plus if there were an illuminating example of
a female disciple in the New Testament who exhibited deep
commitment to the Lord and a very positive impact on her
family members.

Such a model does exist. As will be seen in this chapter,
Eunice (2 Tim. 1:5)—the mother of Timothy, Paul's
younger ministry associate (Acts 16:1–3)—fits the bill perfectly. Also, since it is known that Eunice's mother, Lois,
was also a Christian (2 Tim. 1:5), it is possible to consider
the spiritual domino effect that discipleship in the family
can have, even when only one parent is a disciple of Christ.

Unfortunately, the biblical material available to help understand the mixed spiritual home of Eunice is not as extensive
as might be hoped. Only Acts 16:1–3 and 2 Timothy 1:5
and 3:10–15 provide hard data.[2] In addition, helpful infer-
ences can be drawn from Acts 18:23, Hebrews 13:23, plus
various passages where the father-son spiritual relationship
between Paul and Timothy is discussed[3] (e.g., Phil. 2:19–24).

Introducing a Crucial Young Disciple

As Paul's second missionary journey was about to commence, the apostle had a serious falling-out with his long-time comrade, Barnabas. What was at issue was whether John Mark, who had deserted them on their first missionary journey (Acts 15:36–40; see 13:13), would get a second chance in his former role as their ministry assistant.[4] Barnabas wanted to let Mark try again, but Paul strongly disagreed. So they went their separate ways, Barnabas with Mark and Paul teaming up with Silas, formerly a leader in the church at Jerusalem (15:22, 39–40).

However, Paul still needed someone to take over the responsibilities that Mark had undertaken previously. Who could he find with the ability to do that job?

One of the worst incidents in Paul's ministry up to that point had been his near-death by stoning in Lystra in Central Asia Minor on his first missionary journey (Acts 14:19–20). Certainly a return to that city would have dredged up most troubling memories. Amazingly, though, this place of Paul's near demise turned out to be the home of the apostle's next assistant. His name was Timothy, and his background was like that of none other who was involved in the Christian mission in Acts.

The reader's introduction to Timothy is found in Acts 16:1–3. That brief introductory portion also alludes to the woman disciple who had a formative impact on Timothy, as well as to the mixed marriage that was certainly a spiritual obstacle he had to overcome to reach the point of relative maturity at which Paul chose him to be involved in ministry. Table 12 reflects how Luke, the author of Acts, arranged the mirroring structure of Acts 16:1–3 to emphasize these points.

The outer layer (vv. 1a and 3b) of this construction reminds Luke's readers of what had happened in that area only months earlier: a nearly fatal stoning at the hands of the Jews in Lystra (14:19–20). The second layer (16:1b and

Table 12
Inverted Structure of Acts 16:1–3

A. (16:1a) Paul arrives in Derbe, then Lystra
   B. (16:1b) There was a special disciple there named Timothy
      C. (16:1c) Timothy was from a (doubly) mixed marriage
      C'. (16:2) Yet Timothy had an exemplary reputation
         among local Christians
   B'. (16:3a) This special disciple was selected to work with
      Paul
A'. (16:3b) Paul has Timothy circumcised because of the local
      Jews' knowledge of Timothy's father's background

16:3a) spotlights Timothy's discipleship and how that qualified him for the role of Paul's assistant. It is the inner layer of the inversion (vv. 1c, 2) that is both its main point and the location of the most important information for a better understanding of discipleship related to women, as will be seen below.

Before considering the decisive female disciple in Timothy's life, it is relevant to this overall study of women as disciples to consider the importance that Luke placed on Timothy. When that is understood, the role of Timothy's mother in discipling him is seen to be all the more critical.

Luke introduces Timothy, "And behold, a certain disciple was there, named Timothy" (16:1). Levinsohn notes, "Major participants in Koine Greek narrative are introduced in three typical ways: (a) in a non-active way in a clause with a non-event verb like *eimi*, 'to be'; (b) with *tis* attributive to a noun phrase; and/or (c) in an active way to an existing scene in connection with *idou*, 'behold.'"[5] It is significant that *all three* techniques of introducing major participants are found in Luke's introduction of Timothy:

1. *Was* is a translation of the non-event verb.
2. *Certain* is a *tis* attributive.
3. *Behold* prefaces the first reference to Timothy.

It is clear that Luke considers young Timothy to be very much a major player on Paul's team from that point forward. But how did Timothy come to the point of being recognized as a highly significant disciple?

The Son of a Female Jewish Believer

In the New Testament era it was considered more important who your father was than your mother. Yet Luke sees fit to mention Timothy's mother first: "Timothy, the son of a Jewish woman who was a believer, but his father was a Greek" (16:1).

Why this exceptional order in introducing Timothy's parents? Probably the best clue to Luke's infraction is seen in regard to how he handles the references to two of Paul's other coworkers in Acts 18. When first mentioned, the name of Aquila is placed before that of his wife, Priscilla (Acts 18:2). Later references, though, are phrased "Priscilla and Aquila" (18:18, 26). Baker concludes, "The reversal of the names . . . may imply that Priscilla was spiritually dominant, so far as knowledge and ministry are concerned."[6]

In the case of Timothy's parents, his mother was almost surely also spiritually dominant, since the silence about his father's spiritual status implies that he was a non-Christian.[7] But, an additional important aspect may be missed because Timothy is introduced as an important "disciple," while his mother is merely called "a believer" (16:1).

That additional piece of information is provided by 2 Timothy 1:5. There the reader finds out that Timothy's mother, Eunice, came to faith in Jesus Christ *before* Timothy (as did his Jewish grandmother, Lois). Perhaps that sequence also implies that Eunice's conversion and testimony was a strong influence on Timothy becoming a Christian.

On the other hand, it does not seem that Eunice actually led Timothy to Christ, since Timothy is frequently called Paul's "child in the Lord" (1 Cor. 4:17), a "child serving his father" (i.e., Paul; Phil. 2:22), and Paul's "son" (2 Tim. 1:2). That almost certainly means that Paul was the one who spoke the gospel message that Timothy responded to with saving faith.

Thus it seems likely that Eunice's influence toward Timothy's conversion took place in the limited time frame related to Acts 14:6–23. Since Timothy is already an exemplary "disciple" in Acts 16:1, near the beginning of Paul's second missionary journey, that would mean that he must have been converted on the first missionary journey in Acts 14.

Possibly Eunice was among the first ones who came to saving faith in Lystra, then Timothy among the latter converts before Paul's stoning, which forced the apostle to leave town. Or possibly Eunice responded the first time Paul came through Lystra, then Timothy did when Paul came back several months later, "strengthening the souls of the disciples" and appointing leadership in each of the new local churches (14:21–23).

Either way, of course, presents a relatively brief window of time. Therefore, the change in Eunice's life after she became a Christian must have been immediate and profound. Though it's impossible to know exactly what those attitudinal and behavioral changes were, it is a safe guess that they would have been manifestations of the "fruit of the Spirit": "love, joy, peace, patience, kindness, goodness, faithfulness, gentleness, self-control" (Gal. 5:22–23).

The Product of a Doubly Mixed Marriage

Had Timothy's family lived in Palestine or many other parts of the Roman Empire, the marriage between Eunice, a Jewess, and Timothy's Greek father would have been totally scandalous. But there is evidence that in Central Asia Minor, where Lystra is located, "there can be little doubt that the Jews married into the dominant families."[8]

Thus, there is a strong likelihood that Eunice's family (i.e., almost certainly her father)[9] arranged her marriage into a prominent local Greek family. That would have provided Eunice with significant wealth and social prominence in the Greek community. But it would still have made for uneasy relations with the Jews who lived in the area. Even if they accepted such a marriage from a pragmatic perspective, the normal Jewish outlook on Gentiles (i.e., as "dogs") surely still applied somewhat.

In certain respects it would seem that a wife and mother in such a family would normally have relatively little influence. After all, it was a strongly male-dominant society. Further, if the family was of some financial means, there were servants (or slaves) who handled many of the duties of a wife and mother in a nuclear family of the day. Also, Eunice had married into the prevailing Greek culture and society and would be expected to be considerably hellenized (i.e., taking on Greek ways) herself as well as her children.

Apparently, though, there was a tenacity in Eunice that would not let go of the core of her Jewish beliefs, in spite of her ethnically mixed marriage. Paul's revealing statement to Timothy, "from childhood you have known the sacred writings" (2 Tim. 3:15), indicates that she was determined to pass on the Old Testament Scriptures as the source of those beliefs to her children.

It is not possible to know for sure why Eunice was so tenacious. But two virtually opposite possibilities exist, either of which would have fueled her commitment to convert Timothy in the Old Testament faith:

1. If wider Judaism of the day (whether or not in Central Asia Minor) considered a Jew marrying a Gentile nonlegal, then any children would be viewed as Jewish. Thus, the Jewish parent would have the responsibility to raise the children as Jews.[10]

2. If there was a more flexible outlook among the Jews, or if Timothy was considered Gentile because of his father or lack of circumcision,[11] that still would not necessarily blunt Eunice's determination. In fact, she would probably have redoubled her efforts to keep Timothy from becoming just another Greek boy growing up in the Greek Lystra of that day.

It can be clearly seen that even before Eunice became a Christian through the apostle Paul's preaching, there was more than the tension of a mere ethnically mixed marriage at work in her home. There was also already a very different spiritual perspective: the Old Testament Scriptures, which Eunice apparently clung to, versus whatever Greek philosophy or religion her husband embraced.

Then Paul came to town. Soon Eunice and her mother, Lois, had both been converted by Paul's message (2 Tim. 1:5). At that point, the differences that had simmered throughout the marriage likely came to a boil. It would have been the fruit of the Spirit in Eunice's life along with her desire to give stability to her children and to convert her husband to her new faith in Jesus Christ that would have motivated her. Yet her odds of accomplishing the latter in a heavily Greek and male-dominant society were small.

Suffice it to say that it took considerable patience and wisdom for Eunice to handle her doubly mixed marriage. For all the ethnic/cultural difference, though, it was likely the vast spiritual chasm between herself and her husband that was the most difficult, especially in her desire to worship the Lord and to teach her children about him.

Highly Respected by the Local Christians

Even Luke's description of Timothy as "well spoken of by the brethren who were in Lystra and Iconium" (Acts 16:2) undoubtedly owed a great deal to Eunice's influence.

After all, how would it be possible for Timothy to come to the point of being singled out as an exemplary disciple in no more than a year and a half[12] between his conversion on Paul's first missionary journey (Acts 14:8–23) and when the apostle returned near the beginning of his second mission tour (16:1–3)?

It would seem that Timothy had a very strong spiritual foundation on which to build: his knowledge of the Scripture (2 Tim. 3:15), largely due to Eunice, and a godly example that strongly impacted him, from both Eunice and Lois (2 Tim. 1:5). These would have been challenging accomplishments in the life of a child whose father apparently stood for a very different set of values.

When Timothy became a Christian, these background factors likely helped him to progress very quickly as a disciple. That was certainly what happened in my own life. As a child growing up, I had not come to saving faith in Jesus Christ in the liberal church in which my family was involved. But the influence to memorize Bible verses from both my mother (who was already a Christian) and my step-grandmother (who was a godly woman) got me ready for when I did come to the Lord.

I will not claim that my motives in learning Scripture were as pure as Timothy's. Often it was the bribes of candy or money that lit the fire under me to learn those verses. But learn them I did.

Most of that took place during my preteen years. Yet amazingly, when I became a Christian at the beginning of my senior year in college (soon after my twenty-first birthday), I still remembered all those biblical passages. Some, like the Ten Commandments, Psalm 23, and 1 Corinthians 13 were extended sections, but I recalled them as if I had memorized them the day before.

What an advantage. In even the very first Bible studies I attended after my conversion, I found myself remember-

ing all kinds of relevant verses—usually without even looking them up. (Frankly, that was most helpful because I didn't
even know where in the Bible many of the books were
located.) It really motivated me to get moving in my deeper
study of God's Word and made the adjustment to seminary
after only two years as a believer much easier.

Timothy's growth in his initial period as a Christian,
however, makes me look like a slacker. All I did was progress
to the point of being able to qualify spiritually for admit-
tance into a preparatory seminary program.

By contrast, at an even younger age (probably eighteen
to twenty)[13] Timothy displayed the kind of exemplary qualities that are to be expected of older, mature leaders. That
can be seen in the term Luke chooses to describe Timothy's reputation with the believers in Lystra and Iconium.
The Greek word *martureo*, translated "well spoken of" (Acts
16:2) is the same word used to lay out a qualification for
the seven new leaders to be chosen in the Jerusalem church
in Acts 6:3, where it is rendered "good reputation."[14] That
implies that Timothy's maturity and consistency of character and behavior were at least gradually comparable to
those seven leaders selected in Acts 6, who included
Stephen and Philip (6:5).

With Honor Comes Pain

It was, undoubtedly, a source of great joy to Eunice that
Timothy had grown in Christ so rapidly and with such balance. His excellent reputation among all the Christian
brothers and sisters in the area would have been a dream
come true after raising Timothy in a difficult mixed-mar-
riage home (Acts 16:1–2).

The apostle Paul's return to Lystra brought an additional
compliment regarding Timothy, but, unfortunately, that
highest compliment caused mixed emotions. Paul thought

so much of Timothy's progress and character that he decided to ask Timothy to "go with him" (16:3) as a ministry assistant.

Sorrow of Parting

It was a high honor to receive that invitation from such a judge of character as Paul. However, it would mean that young Timothy would likely be geographically distant from his family for an extended length of time—possibly for the rest of his life.

What a quandary for this godly mother. She had poured so much of her pre-Christian married life into exposing her children to Hebrew Scriptures (2 Tim. 3:15). Then, after she became a believer (2 Tim. 1:5), she undoubtedly prayed fervently for her son, that he also would come to faith in Jesus Christ. She had certainly also been there to support and encourage him during his earliest stages of Christian growth, and she had reason to praise God as his progress and giftedness (see 1 Tim. 4:14)[15] shattered all expectations.

Working with Paul, however, was a different matter. After all, the "St. Paul Worldwide Evangelism and Church Planting Ministry" was not exactly a safe organization with which to have your employment. The first missionary journey in Central Asia Minor had been characterized by staying one step ahead of the Jews who wanted to stop Paul and the gospel, until the Jews caught up to Paul in Lystra and tried to kill him by stoning (Acts 14:19–20). In her mind's eye, Eunice could still see the angry bruises and cuts that marred Paul's appearance as he barely managed to get up and walk away from that terrible ordeal (14:20).

If Timothy went with Paul, he could very possibly be stoned also. At best, colaboring with Paul in ministry was a calculated risk. Paul was one of those people whom others usually loved or hated. And Timothy would be right there with Paul when those who hated the apostle would seek to stop his ministry and/or end his life.

Yet Timothy did go with Paul. As the first less than fully Jewish member of the apostle's missionary band, Timothy would have a great impact as they increasingly ministered to heavily Gentile communities. Further, it is quite likely that Luke focuses on Timothy because Timothy's participation with Paul paved the way for a fully Gentile person, like himself, to begin working with the apostle.[16]

Choosing Circumcision

There would have been another difficult decision in connection with Paul's request for Timothy to accompany him in his missionary endeavors. Because of his Greek father, Timothy had never been circumcised (Acts 16:3). It apparently would have been an affront to his father or his father's family. But Paul convinced Timothy that the possible reaction of the Jewish community to an uncircumcised man could be strong and unfortunate.

While Eunice would have come around quickly to seeing that Timothy's being circumcised was the wise, expedient thing to do for the sake of the gospel, two other powerful feelings would surely have come into play:

1. Painful memories would have flooded back of her struggle when her boy baby had not been allowed by his father to be circumcised in keeping with the Jewish law (Gen. 17:9–14).
2. Being circumcised as an adult was a painful, debilitating procedure that would have laid him up for a period of several days.[17]

Eunice's regret and her compassion for her hurting child (even though he was a young adult) would have dominated her thoughts and feelings, even as she was preparing to say farewell to her son for an undetermined length of time.

Brief Reunion

If Eunice was a normal loving mother, she likely began counting the days until Timothy returned to Lystra on the day that he left. There was a good possibility that Timothy had never ventured far from home. Thus not only the possible danger but just the very absence of her beloved son would have been difficult.

Perhaps Eunice's expectations in regard to how soon she would see Timothy were not very realistic either. Probably Paul assured her that he would return to visit the churches in her area just as soon as it was practical to do so. However, Paul probably had not yet considered the possibility of doing evangelism and church planting in Europe on the second missionary journey (Acts 16:9–10). Thus the duration of their missions tour grew from a likely period of months, as with the first missionary journey, to at least two years.

Along the way, it is possible that Timothy wrote home to keep Eunice apprised of what was happening.[18] If so, the Macedonian vision and the mixed responses to the gospel in Northern and Southern Greece would have been known to her, and she would have been amazed at what the Lord was doing through his servants Paul, Silas, and Timothy. If not, Eunice certainly still prayed fervently for her son and the others on a regular basis.

When Timothy finally came back to Lystra, it was just for a brief visit (Acts 18:23). Paul had seen fit to begin his third mission tour virtually exactly the same way he had the second journey (15:41–16:1). He revisited the churches that had been originally founded on the first journey in Timothy's home area (Acts 14), "strengthening all the disciples" (18:23). So even though it was at best a short working vacation, Timothy did have the opportunity to see Eunice, Lois, and the other Christians of the area who thought so highly of him.

What a joyful family reunion that must have been. Since there were probably unbelievers in the immediate family—on Eunice's side because of their Jewishness and with the entire Greek side of Timothy's unbelieving father (16:1, 3)—the strongest loving family context that Timothy went home to was his "brethren" in Christ (16:2). The days (or few weeks) when Timothy was present would have been filled with sharing what the Lord was doing all over the Greek homeland, from Timothy, and person-by-person in the immediate area, from Eunice and the other Christians in Lystra.

Then the day came for Timothy to leave again. As Eunice and Timothy embraced and wished each other the Lord's best, both were probably projecting ahead to the point when Timothy could return for another visit. Insofar as the Scriptures reveal the movement of Timothy's ministry in the time ahead, though, that was not to be.[19]

Hurting When Your Child Hurts

It was not long before Paul began a nearly three-year ministry in the great city of Ephesus, several hundred miles southwest of Lystra (Acts 19:1–10; 20:31). If Timothy was occasionally writing Eunice, or if he got home again during that time, he would have told of the remarkable things the Lord was doing throughout the Roman province of Asia (19:10).

All was not to be joyful in the time ahead for Paul's ministry, however. There was a dangerous riot in Ephesus at the end of their time there (Acts 19:23–20:1). Then Paul was falsely arrested in Jerusalem and was behind bars in Jerusalem, Caesarea, and Rome for four years (Acts 24:27; 28:30) before being released.[20]

All the while, Timothy's assignments as Paul's representative were getting progressively more difficult. He was, for example, sent by the apostle to mediate a difficult dispute in the church at Philippi (Phil. 2:19–23; 4:2–3). Then, after Paul was free again, Timothy was left in Ephesus to serve a sort of interim pastorate there because of the apostle's deep, ongoing concern in respect to the impact of false teaching (1 Tim. 1:3) in the church he had worked with longest in his three journeys (Acts 20:28–31).

All of these tasks would have greatly concerned Eunice, to whatever extent she knew about them, but Timothy's plight in Ephesus was likely the most troubling. Back in Lystra Timothy had been the boy wonder, the spiritual prodigy who had earned the respect of all the local believers as well as the apostle Paul's attention (Acts 16:2–3). But in Ephesus, without Paul's immediate authority backing him up, Timothy was being discounted as too young[21] to fill the role assigned to him by Paul (1 Tim. 4:12).

Over a period of time, likely two or three years,[22] the external dangers related to false teaching and the internal criticism apparently beat Timothy down and left him in a depressed state. That Paul used references to the faith of Eunice and Lois (2 Tim. 1:5) to motivate his beloved lieutenant in ministry seems to indicate how deeply he respected their discipleship and that both women were alive and well and going on in the Lord.

This reference implies a very down-to-earth, two-way relationship. On the one hand, Timothy could be heartened by the long-term godly examples of his mother and grandmother, mature disciples that they were. On the other hand, Eunice would have been deeply concerned about her son, who was for now a near casualty of the ministry. She certainly would have loved to be there to help "bear one another's burdens" (Gal. 6:2), one Christian to another. But even deeper, she could not deny her pain as a mother and her desire to comfort her downcast son.

Unfortunately, things did not soon improve much, even though Paul asked Timothy to leave Ephesus and come to Rome as soon as possible (2 Tim. 4:9–13). Apparently, some time after Timothy's arrival in Rome, he was also arrested and not released until after Caesar Nero's death (Heb. 13:23). Since strong tradition outside the Bible holds that Nero killed both Paul and Peter before his own death in A.D. 68, that means Timothy's life was also in danger.

Can you imagine the deeply mixed emotions that Eunice must have felt upon learning of Timothy's trip to join Paul, then his imprisonment and personal danger, and the death of her dear friend Paul? Her situation was very similar to a mother sending her son off to war, because ultimately the Christian life and ministry are warfare—usually unseen spiritual warfare (2 Cor. 10:3–5; Eph. 6:10–18; 2 Tim. 2:3–4).

Being Discipled by Eunice

There is a saying, "Behind every great man you'll find a great woman." Typically, that applies first to the man's wife. But in many cases it should apply equally to his mother.

Why? If Christian psychologists are correct in concluding that the vast majority of a child's personality is determined by the time he or she is six years old, it is simple to figure out that the mother (or in too many cases today, the child-care provider) is the crucial formative influence in those early years. What she does or does not do in regard to teaching moral truth by word and example and whether the child is initially exposed to God's Word and God's people may well be pivotal to that growing person's entire lifetime.

Make no mistake about it, if the mother is a disciple of Jesus Christ, she is embodying her commitment to the Lord by discipling her children. As the example of Eunice shows so well, even if such a female disciple finds herself in the midst of a very trying mixed marriage, it is possible through various means to have a decisive impact for godliness on her children. The difficulty of such circumstances should never be underestimated, but the rewards should not be underestimated either. The joy and satisfaction of "Well done, good and faithful servant" will last eternally.

Without the female disciple Eunice, there likely would not have been a Timothy to take up the slack on Paul's second missionary journey. Similarly it is worth wondering what "Eunices" will be eternally commended by the Lord for helping disciple the "Timothys" needed in the Lord's service until Christ returns.

Twelve

WOMEN AS DISCIPLES
Then and Now

This study of the female disciples in the New Testament has been an eye-opening, challenging, and sometimes heart-wrenching, experience.[1] As important as each individual discussion has been, we would like to conclude with an overview of the women disciples as a group. As is so often true, "the whole is greater than the sum of the parts" in the case of women disciples in the New Testament.

Certainly Mary, the mother of Jesus, played many roles in the New Testament record. She was first a young disciple caught in the confusing circumstances of her supernatural pregnancy and then the mother of the Messiah. She had to watch her beloved be rejected and crucified as a falsely accused criminal. But then came the joyous realization of his resurrected and ascended glory and his founding of his church (Matt. 16:18).

Elizabeth and Anna only make cameo appearances, but the courage and character they both display mark them as very valuable veteran disciples for our study and emulation. Similarly only limited New Testament material informs us about courageous Mary Magdalene (and the other female disciples present at the cross and tomb of Jesus) or the Samaritan woman—a societally unacceptable female disciple. Yet there is enough data to be able to perceive how each forged her commitment to the Lord Jesus Christ on the anvil of her unique personal circumstances.

Mary and Martha of Bethany had close friendships with Jesus, hosting him often in their home. But their discipleship reminds us of how different disciples who live under the same roof can be and that even such drastically different personalities still react to the Lord in the same way.

Dorcas, Priscilla, Phoebe, and several of the women disciples in Philippi all reflect various kinds of significant, informal servant-leader roles in the churches in which they were involved.[2] On the other hand, other than Priscilla (and possibly Junia),[3] Eunice and the women in the church in Rome seemed to play lower-profile positions. Since women today find themselves in roles parallel to all of them, each contributes invaluably to our understanding of women as disciples.

The remarkable and inspiring lives of Mary, Elizabeth, Mary Magdalene, Mary of Bethany, Martha, Dorcas, Priscilla, Lydia, and the others each show us certain characteristics and lessons that need to be applied by disciples at the end of the twentieth century. When all those points are stacked up together, it is immediately seen that female disciples in the New Testament record are outstanding examples to us. They were all intended by the Divine Author of Scripture to be timeless[4] models (even indirect mentors of a sort) for every future generation of disciples. Each woman would undoubtedly be delighted to know that you had profited from her particular example of discipleship.

The New Testament does not show us what these women looked like physically, how tall they were, or the color of their eyes. What we do see, though, are the attitudes and actions that characterized the discipleship of these incredible women. Table 13 lists thirty items that are at the heart of the New Testament portrayal of women as disciples.

Table 13
Major New Testament Expressions for Women as Disciples

Anointing Jesus generously (to be remembered wherever the gospel spreads)	Matt. 26:6–13; Mark 14:3–9; John 12:1–8; see also Luke 7:36–50
Followers	Matt. 27:55; Mark 15:41; Luke 23:49
Waiting on Jesus	Matt. 27:55; Mark 15:41
Believing (initial) witnesses of the resurrection	Matt. 28:1–10; Mark 16:1–11; Luke 24:1–10; John 20:1–18
Filled with the Holy Spirit and speaking	Luke 1:41–42; see also Eph. 5:18–19
Prophesying	Luke 2:36; see also Acts 21:9; 1 Cor. 11:5
Fasting and prayer	Luke 2:37
With Jesus	Luke 8:1–2
Contributing financially to support ministry	Luke 8:3
Sitting at the Lord's feet, listening	Luke 10:39
Carrying the cross, counting the cost, etc.	Luke 14:26–33
Giving personal testimony of Jesus	John 4:28–39
Continuing in prayer	Acts 1:13–14; 2:42
Full of good works and acts of mercy	Acts 9:36
Hosting the church (prayer meeting/ house church)	Acts 12:12; 16:14–15, 40; Rom. 16:3, 5
Being a faithful, believing mother	Acts 16:1–3; 1 Tim. 2:15; 2 Tim. 1:5, 3:15

continued

(Table 13—continued)
Major New Testament Expressions for Women as Disciples

Correcting a male leader/ preacher (privately)	Acts 18:24–26
Deaconess or servant of the church	Rom. 16:1
Helper or good friend to many	Rom. 16:2
Fellow worker	Rom. 16:3; Phil. 4:3
Hard worker	Rom. 16:6, 12
Outstanding among the apostles (possibly)	Rom. 16:7
Use of spiritual gifts	1 Cor. 12, 14
"Sons" of God through faith in Christ	Gal. 3:26; 4:5–7
"Neither male nor female" in Christ, coheirs of promise	Gal. 3:28–29
Roles as wife, mother	Eph. 5:22–6:9; Col. 3:16–4:1
Sharing in the struggle of the gospel	Phil. 4:3
Widows indeed	1 Tim. 5:3–16; see also Luke 2:36–38; Acts 9:36–41
Teaching/training younger women	Titus 2:3–5
Overcomers/victors (promises to each of the churches)	Rev. 2–3; 21:7

We remain very much in awe of the courageous commitment, character, and achievements of the female New Testament disciples assembled in this book and summarized in table 13. It is our hope that you will consistently pull out this list and review it in order to gain further insight and be challenged anew as a disciple.

Though the list is not exhaustive, it is complete enough to make it clear that the distinctive New Testament portrait of women as disciples, though overlapping with that of male disciples at a number of points, is many-faceted. The working out of these aspects of discipleship runs the gamut from low-profile to high-profile, from home to friendships and from outreach to corporate ministry. They frequently include deep struggle and pain, as well as joy and fulfillment.

What it all boils down to, though, is personally growing more daily into the image of Jesus Christ, to whom all Christians owe their full allegiance as disciples (Luke 14:26–33). That is also closely linked with enabling other disciples to do likewise throughout life or until he returns (Matt. 28:19–20). Being a growing disciple and reproducing disciples is the great practical challenge that the Lord has placed before both female and male disciples. That is the two-pronged goal that must be passionately pursued in unison by disciples of both genders and all evangelical positions.[5] So let's get on with it—together!

NOTES

Introduction

1. This phrase was used by some discipleship practitioners in the early to mid 1980s to refer to the unparalleled interest in discipleship that had mushroomed during the 1970s, predominantly in the United States.

2. Michael J. Wilkins, *Following the Master: Discipleship in the Footsteps of Jesus* (Grand Rapids: Zondervan, 1992).

3. See, e.g., Kathy McReynolds, "Elizabeth," "Martha," "Mary, the Mother of Jesus," "Mary Magdalene," "The Samaritan Woman," and "Susanna," in *The Complete Who's Who of the Bible,* ed. Paul Gardner (Grand Rapids: Zondervan, 1995). A recent scholarly treatment by an evangelical is Grant R. Osborne, "Women in Jesus' Ministry," *Westminster Theological Journal* 51 (1989): 259–91.

4. See also Kathy McReynolds, "Priscilla," in *The Complete Who's Who of the Bible,* ed. Gardner. For a more scholarly treatment, see A. Boyd Luter, "Partners in the Gospel: the Role of Women in the Church at Philippi," *Journal of the Evangelical Theological Society* (1997); and "Tabitha/Dorcas: A Model Disciple?" (paper presented at the Evangelical Theological Society, Far West Region, Sun Valley, Calif., April 1994).

5. See the discussions in A. Boyd Luter, "Discipleship and the Church," *Bibliotheca Sacra* (July-Sept. 1980): 167–73; and A. Boyd Luter, *A New Testament Theology of Discipling* (Ann Arbor: University Microfilms, 1985).

6. These fresh angles were essentially unanticipated because of the extensive survey of the women in the New Testament, including their roles as disciples to a significant degree, that was undertaken in the early chapters of Ruth A. Tucker and Walter L. Liefeld, *Daughters of the Church: Women and Ministry from New Testament Times to the Present* (Grand Rapids: Academie/Zondervan, 1987).

7. For example, the known feminist sympathies of both Ruth Tucker and Walter Liefeld clearly colored the (often useful) material argued in *Daughters of the Church* as, at best, highly questionable in many more conservative (and traditionalist) evangelical circles.

8. Boyd Luter was Associate Editor/Biblical for the *Life Recovery Bible*, ed. David Stoop and Steve Arterburn (Wheaton: Tyndale, 1992), to which Kathy McReynolds contributed. McReynolds and Luter coauthored "Recovering Through Fully Biblical Recovery," *Christian Research Journal* (Spring 1993); and *Truthful Living: What Scripture Really Teaches About Recovery* (Grand Rapids: Baker, 1994).

9. See notes 3 and 4 above and Kathy McReynolds, "Hannah" and "Aquila," in *The Complete Who's Who of the Bible*, ed. Gardner.

10. A. Boyd Luter, "Zechariah (NT)" and "Joseph of Arimathea," in *The Complete Who's Who of the Bible*, ed. Gardner.

11. A. Boyd Luter, "Great Commission," in *Anchor Bible Dictionary*, 6 vols., gen. ed. David Noel Freedman (Garden City, N.Y.: Doubleday, 1992). See note five above and the selected bibliography at the end of the book for dissertation and article data.

Chapter 1: *Unexpected Disciples and the Great Commission*

1. See A. Boyd Luter, "Discipleship and the Church," *Bibliotheca Sacra* (1980): 267–73; and Luter, *Theology of Discipling*.

2. For a brief discussion of the overall New Testament usage, see A. Boyd Luter, "Great Commission," 2:1090–91.

3. In this introductory chapter, only the *presence* of women disciples will be nailed down. Several of the later chapters will develop what is known about the women seen in these passages in more depth and in regard to the practical personal aspects of their lives. For a somewhat similar survey that partly focuses on women as disciples, see chapters 1 and 2 of Tucker and Liefeld, *Daughters of the Church*.

4. Though Mark 16:9–20 is found in the vast majority of the surviving Greek manuscripts, it is not present in several of the older man-

uscripts. Thus, many leading scholars doubt that it is original. For compact wisdom in dealing with such text critical matters, see David Alan Black's recent *New Testament Criticism: A Concise Guide* (Grand Rapids: Baker, 1994).

5. "Make disciples" is the lone command to which the three participles (*going, baptizing,* and *teaching*) relate, meaning that the participles explain how the command is to be worked out in practice.

6. A helpful explanation of what was involved in these women disciples following Jesus can be found in David M. Scholer, "Women," in *Dictionary of Jesus and the Gospels,* ed. Joel Green, Scot McKnight, and Howard Marshall (Downers Grove, Ill.: InterVarsity Press, 1992), 882.

7. The only other mention of baptism in Matthew deals with John the Baptist baptizing Jesus (3:13–17), which is certainly not identical in meaning to Christian baptism, as is seen clearly in Acts 18:25; 19:3–5.

8. Inverted, or chiastic, structures emphasize points in two ways: (1) by parallelism (i.e., mirroring ideas) in the first and second halves of the structure, and (2) the point focused on at the middle of the structure. Luter has worked extensively with the meaning of such structures. See e.g., A. Boyd Luter and Barry C. Davis, *God Behind the Seen: Expositions of Ruth and Esther,* Expositor's Guides to the Historical Books (Grand Rapids: Baker, 1995); and A. Boyd Luter and Michelle V. Lee, "Philippians as Chiasmus: Key to the Structure, Unity and Theme Questions," *New Testament Studies* (1995).

9. Jesus' earlier debate with the Sadducees over the resurrection (Matt. 22:23–33) indicates it was commonly believed by many Jews that bodies would be resurrected at the end time, based on Daniel 12:1–2.

10. It is quite likely that, through the combination of the usage of the idea of service (27:55) and the mention of "the mother of the sons of Zebedee" (27:56), Matthew is recalling Jesus' earlier linking of such service and true greatness among his followers (Matt. 20:26–28) in reply to the brash request of "the mother of the sons of Zebedee" (20:20).

11. If this proposed literary structure of Matthew 27:50–28:20 is correct, the "end of the age" (28:20) links the final fulfillment of the Great Commission to the general time period of the resurrection at the end of the age (27:52–53; see Dan. 12:2). In that regard, it may be significant that the book of Daniel concludes with the prophet Daniel being told that he would be resurrected "at the end of the age" (Dan. 12:13).

12. This assumes that Salome (Mark 15:40) is also "the mother of the sons of Zebedee" (Matt. 27:56), the most common evangelical view.

13. For a compact discussion of what is known about this "eleventh-hour disciple" from all four gospels, see Luter, "Joseph of Arimathea."

14. Many evangelicals have seen the servanthood of Jesus as a key idea of the second Gospel (see Mark 10:45). If that conclusion is legitimate, the center of this structure fits beautifully with that theme.

15. A different perspective held by some scholars is discussed in Tucker and Liefeld, *Daughters of the Church*, 474–75, note 66.

16. It is virtually certain that this passage is referring to the destruction of Jerusalem in A.D. 70 because of the wording of the Olivet Discourse about women (Luke 21:23) in the midst of describing that destruction.

17. The most common evangelical understanding of the identity of the "beloved disciple" is that it was the apostle John, the author of the fourth Gospel, referring to himself in terms of the wonder of Christ's love for him.

18. Tucker and Liefeld, *Daughters of the Church*, 63, hold that the presence of the women in Acts 1 and the wording of 2:1 ("they were all together in one place") cinches the presence of the women disciples when the Holy Spirit initially descended (2:2–4). Such a conclusion, however, is not clear from the biblical text.

19. It is possible that this prominence is due to the later roles of James and Jude, two of Jesus' brothers through Mary, their common parent (Matt. 13:55). Both became writers of Scripture, and James was a prominent leader of the Jerusalem church (Acts 15:13–21; 21:18; Gal. 1:19; 2:9). But, that still does not explain why the women disciples were even mentioned, and especially, *before* the brothers!

20. Thomas R. Schreiner, "Luke," in *Evangelical Commentary on the Bible*, ed. Walter A. Elwell (Grand Rapids: Baker, 1989), 826.

21. Gary Burge, "John," in *Evangelical Commentary on the Bible*, ed. Elwell, 858, draws the balanced conclusion that, while John 7:53–8:11 was not an original part of the fourth Gospel, it is an authentic saying of Jesus and should be treated as possessing such authority.

Chapter 2: *Mary*

1. For a more in-depth discussion on Roman Catholic theology concerning Mary, see John H. Leith, ed., *Creeds of the Churches*, 3d ed.,

(Louisville: John Knox Press, 1982), 399–484. The doctrine of Mary in the Catholic church is quite involved and complex. Not all Catholics agree with the church's doctrine.

2. For a helpful discussion on women in Israel at the time of Christ, see Alfred Edersheim, *Sketches of Jewish Social Life in the Days of Christ* (Grand Rapids: Eerdmans, 1990), 139–60.

3. For an in-depth treatment of the genealogical records of Matthew and Luke, see D. A. Carson, "Matthew," and Walter L. Liefeld, "Luke," in *Expositor's Bible Commentary,* vol. 8, gen. ed., Frank E. Gaebelein (Grand Rapids: Zondervan, 1984), 61–69, 861–62.

4. Liefeld, "Luke," 830. He also points out that this same Greek word is used in Eph. 1:6, where the apostle Paul implies that this grace is given to all believers.

5. Tucker and Liefeld, *Daughters of the Church,* 19.

6. See also McReynolds, "Elizabeth."

7. Mary's was, of course, a supernatural conception, but so was Elizabeth's, since she was past the childbearing years (Luke 1:7).

8. The title, the Magnificat, is attributed to Jerome's translation of Luke 1:46. For an in-depth discussion on the structure and purpose of Mary's song, see C. J. Martin, "Mary's Song" in *Dictionary of Jesus and the Gospels,* ed. Green, McKnight, and Marshall, 525–26.

9. Liefeld, "Luke," 835.

10. This is the next event Scripture presents concerning the lives of Mary and Jesus. Nothing is known with certainty about what happened during the intervening twelve years.

11. Tucker and Liefeld, *Daughters of the Church,* 23.

12. The wedding at Cana probably took place at the beginning of Christ's ministry. See Merrill C. Tenney, "The Gospel of John," in *Expositor's Bible Commentary,* vol. 9, ed. Gaebelein, 42.

13. Ibid., 42.

14. A. T. Robertson, *The Mother of Jesus: Her Problems and Her Glory* (Grand Rapids: Baker, 1963), 54.

15. Mary J. Evans, *Woman in the Bible* (Downer's Grove, Ill.: Inter-Varsity Press, 1983), 59–60.

Chapter 3: *Elizabeth and Anna*

1. If Mary was only sixteen or seventeen years old when Jesus was born, she would have been near fifty at the time of his death, assum-

ing that Jesus began his ministry at "about thirty years of age" (Luke 3:23) and had approximately a three-year long ministry (Harold W. Hoehner, "Chronology," in *Dictionary of Jesus and the Gospels*, ed. Green, McKnight, and Marshall, 119). It is quite possible Mary was widowed because that is the most natural explanation of why Joseph is never seen during the public ministry of Jesus.

2. If several examples of older male disciples are desired, Mnason, the veteran disciple (Acts 21:16), Paul, the "old man" (Philem. 9 NIV), and the apostle who lived the longest, John, come immediately to mind.

3. The mention of the Holy Spirit and John's birth, alongside required abstinence from alcoholic beverages, likely echoes the very similar elements in the description of Samson's birth and later development (Judg. 13:4–5, 24–25).

4. It is significant that these are the only three uses of the exact phrase "filled [Greek *pletho*] with the Holy Spirit" in Luke, with only five uses in Acts (2:4; 4:8; 31; 9:17; 13:9).

5. Liefeld, "Luke," 8:803, citing Charles Talbert, refers to "Luke's ability to use the device of chiasm . . . as a major structural means of presenting this message."

6. This similarity would be highly significant in its own right. However, the inclusion of two other less complex chiastic structures in Luke 1 (1:39–45 and 1:57–67), probably parallel to the less complex inverted structure in 23:54–24:49, marks the mirroring nature of the beginning and ending portions of the third Gospel as astounding literary artistry.

7. For another treatment of Zechariah, see A. Boyd Luter, "Zechariah (NT)." Tucker and Liefeld, *Daughters of the Church*, 19, 25, discuss both the comparison of Zechariah and Elizabeth here and the implied contrast between the doubting of the older Zechariah (Luke 1:12–20) and the faith of the much younger Mary (1:29–38).

8. There is no way of knowing whether Elizabeth, who was apparently much older than Mary (Luke 1:7, 27), was her aunt or cousin. Also, it is not known how Elizabeth could be of the "daughters of Aaron" (1:5), from the tribe of Levi, and Mary of the tribe of Judah, as is held by many evangelicals who think that Luke 3 reflects Mary's family tree (e.g., McReynolds in *The Complete Who's Who of the Bible*, 444; see Luke 3:23, 33).

9. This strong inference may provide a key piece of scriptural evidence that has not yet been adequately discussed in the abortion debate.

10. Liefeld, "Luke," 835–36, discusses the various views on the composition of the Magnificat, helpfully assessing Mary's potential for originating such an amazing song.

11. Liefeld, "Luke," 835.

12. The mention of the neighbors and relatives taking part in the naming of the child may reflect an ancient practice in Israel, first seen in Scripture in Ruth 4:17. For further discussion, see A. Boyd Luter, "Ruth."

13. Liefeld, "Luke," 824, speaks of "an atmosphere reminiscent of the OT, with a grammatical and stylistic Semitic cast. . . . The Semitic style fits the religious and historical connection Luke is establishing between the OT and NT periods."

14. Up to this point in the third Gospel, there have been two pairs of characters presented: Zechariah and Elizabeth; Mary and Joseph. It is more than likely that Simeon and Anna, though not married, are intended to portray a "couple" of prophets (note Anna being called a "prophetess" in Luke 2:36 and the repeated mention of the Holy Spirit in relation to Simeon's action in 2:25–27). Tucker and Liefeld, *Daughters of the Church*, 26, assert that, because Jewish Law required the testimony of two witnesses, Anna is the second witness in this passage, although the testimony of women was not acceptable in that society. Given Luke's emphasis on women, that is possible but far from certain.

15. Liefeld, "Luke," 850, traces the idea of "the consolation of Israel" (2:25) back to prophecies of the advent of the Messiah in Isa. 40:1–2; 57:18; 61:2.

16. It is possible that these complementary elements serve as inverted bookends around this passage: "the consolation of Israel" (A) and "the Lord's Christ" (B), being balanced by speaking of him (B′) and "the redemption of Jerusalem" (A′), calling special attention to the significance of the events in the Temple that day (Luke 2:25–38).

17. George W. Knight III, "1 Timothy," in *Evangelical Commentary on the Bible*, ed. Elwell, 1107.

18. Schreiner, "Luke," 809, understands "she never left the temple, serving night and day" (Luke 2:37) as that Anna likely "resided in one of the many rooms adjacent to the temple."

19. For a related discussion on worship, see A. Boyd Luter, "Worship as Service: The New Testament Usage of Latrueo," *Criswell Theological Review* (Spring 1988).

Chapter 4: *Mary Magdalene*

1. For a concise discussion on Mary Magdalene, see Kathy McReynolds, "Mary Magdalene."

2. The village is also referred to as "Magadan" (Matt. 15:39) and "Dalmanutha" (Mark 8:10).

3. Raymond F. Collins, "Mary Magdalene," in *Anchor Bible Dictionary*, vol. 4, ed. Freedman, 579.

4. Clinton Arnold, *Powers of Darkness* (Downers Grove, Ill.: InterVarsity Press, 1992), 21.

5. See also chapter 10 for a discussion on the demon-possessed servant girl in Philippi in Acts 16.

6. Ben Witherington, *Women in the Ministry of Jesus* (Cambridge: Cambridge University Press, 1984), 117–18.

7. Ibid., 121.

8. See chapter 1 for a discussion of the implications of the textual question related to Mark 16:9–20.

9. Tucker and Liefeld, *Daughters of the Church*, 40.

10. However, there does seem to be a bookend effect noted by the repetition of "for fear of the Jews" in John 19:38 and 20:19. See the brief discussion in chapter 1.

11. Elizabeth Tetlow, *Women and Ministry in the New Testament: Called to Serve* (New York: Paulist Press, 1980), 114, 119.

12. For a complementary treatment of how to deal with painful past issues from a biblical perspective, see A. Boyd Luter, *Looking Back, Moving On* (Colorado Springs: NavPress, 1993) and A. Boyd Luter and Kathy McReynolds, *Truthful Living*.

Chapter 5: *Mary and Martha*

1. Scholer, "Women," 880–87.

2. Witherington, *Women in the Ministry of Jesus*, 100–101.

3. The six other signs in John's gospel are changing water to wine at the wedding at Cana, John 2:1–11; healing at the pool, John 5:2–9; feeding the five thousand, John 6:1–14; Jesus walks on the water, John 6:19; and healing of the blind man, John 9:6–7.

4. Note the mention of Bethany in Matt. 26:6; Luke 10:38, 24:50; John 12:1.

5. *The New Westminster Dictionary of the Bible*, ed. Henry Snyder Gehman (Philadelphia: Westminster Press, 1970).

6. Merrill F. Unger, *Unger's Bible Dictionary,* 3d ed., (Chicago: Moody Press, 1985), 138.

7. Jesus was on the east side of the Jordan (John 10:40), which was about twenty miles from Bethany. It could be walked in a day. This accounts for the four-day time lapse in John 11:17—a day for the messenger's journey, a two-day delay (11:6), and Jesus' journey to Bethany. Lazarus must have died shortly after the messenger left.

8. See the discussion in Gary Burge, "John," 864.

9. Elizabeth Tetlow, *Women and Ministry,* 112.

10. Witherington, *Women in the Ministry of Jesus,* 109.

11. For a full discussion of such recovery issues from a theological perspective, see Luter and McReynolds, *Truthful Living.*

12. Tucker and Liefeld, *Daughters of the Church,* 28.

13. For individual treatment of Martha, see Kathy McReynolds, "Martha."

14. Witherington, *Women in the Ministry of Jesus,* 112, 115–16.

Chapter 6: *The Samaritan Woman*

1. It must be understood that John's main purpose for including the Samaritan woman account is not to prove that women can become disciples. His major point for this account is twofold: First, the Messiah, who is the Savior of the world, has the divine ability to search the human heart (John 4:17–19). Second, those who worship God, regardless of their ethnic background, must do so in spirit and in truth (John 4:21–24). These two truths support his overall purpose to prove that Jesus is the Son of God and that believing in him brings eternal life (John 20:31).

2. For a discussion on the Samaritan woman, see McReynolds, "Samaritan Woman." For a discussion on the Samaritan woman from a recovery standpoint, see *Truthful Living.*

3. Merrill C. Tenney, "John," 54.

4. For a concise discussion on the Greek word construction in John 4:4, see A. T. Robertson, *Word Pictures in the New Testament,* vol. 5 (Nashville: Broadman Press, 1932), 59–60.

5. Tenney, "John," 54.

6. When the northern kingdom of Israel fell to the Assyrians in 722 B.C., the king of Assyria deported the Israelites and resettled their land (especially the capital of Israel, Samaria) with peoples of other nations.

These peoples mixed the worship of Yahweh with the worship of their own gods. This syncretic religion of people of Samaria put them at odds with the Jews of the southern kingdom of Judah. They remained arch enemies from that time forward.

7. Craig S. Keener, *The IVP Bible Background Commentary: New Testament* (Downer's Grove, Ill.: InterVarsity Press, 1993), 272.

8. Ibid., 272.

9. For a more in-depth discussion on "living water," see H. A. Ironside, *Addresses on the Gospel of John* (Neptune: Loizeaux Brothers, 1942), 139–43.

10. For more insight on the Samaritan religion and how the woman displayed her knowledge, see Tenney, "John," 54–56.

11. Mary J. Evans, *Woman in the Bible*, 52.

12. Tucker and Liefeld, *Daughters of the Church*, 33.

13. Witherington, *Women in the Ministry of Jesus*, 61.

14. Tetlow, *Women and Ministry*, 112.

15. Witherington, *Women in the Ministry of Jesus*, 63.

Chapter 7: *Tabitha/Dorcas*

1. John Polhill, "Acts," in *New American Commentary* (Nashville: Broadman, 1992), 247, note 58, states that this feminine form for *disciple* (Greek *mathetria*) is "not uncommon in Greek literature" outside the New Testament.

2. Wilkins, *Following the Master*, 249; and Michael J. Wilkins, "Disciples," in *Dictionary of Jesus and the Gospels*, ed. Green, McKnight, and Marshall, 178.

3. It is amazing that, in their otherwise very thorough treatment of New Testament women, Tucker and Liefeld (*Daughters of the Church*, 66–67) only mention Dorcas for less than a paragraph.

4. Most writers only treat Acts 9:31 as concluding the previous section but do not recognize that it is also transitional to the next larger section (9:32–11:18). Although Polhill, "Acts," 244, sees 9:31 as concluding "the Pauline conversion narrative," he does observe that 9:32–43 shows the church's "extension to the coastal towns of Judea."

5. It is highly unlikely that the fact that widows (Greek *cherai*) are mentioned only in Acts in 6:1 and 9:39, 41 is merely coincidental. Rather, it is almost surely an intended comparison between the passages in which Stephen and Dorcas respectively are introduced.

6. Fritz Rienecker, *Linguistic Key to the Greek New Testament,* trans. and ed. Cleon Rogers (Grand Rapids, Zondervan, 1980), 525.

7. Knowing of the resurrection of Lazarus on the fourth day (John 11:17) and of Jesus on the third day, these women were acting in faith.

8. Joel B. Green, "Burial of Jesus," in *Dictionary of Jesus and the Gospels,* ed. Green, McKnight, and Marshall, 89.

9. Polhill, "Acts," 247, states that the distance between Joppa and Lydda was a "three hours journey by foot."

10. Green, "Burial of Jesus," 89.

11. The Greek words for *arise* are different, though: *egeiro* in Mark 5:41 and *anistemi* in Acts 9:40, 41. The presumed basis for comparison would be wording in Aramaic, though it is not possible to be certain which language Peter was speaking in Acts 9:41.

12. Polhill, "Acts," 199, states that the middle voice of *showing* is the nuance that suggests this understanding.

13. The expanded evangelistic opportunity probably explains why Peter "stayed many days in Joppa" (Acts 9:43), setting up the circumstances that soon led to the conversion of Cornelius and his household in Acts 10.

14. See the introductory discussion of the Great Commission terminology in chapter 1. For a more in-depth treatment, see also A. Boyd Luter, "Discipleship and the Church," 167–73.

Chapter 8: *Priscilla*

1. Richard Longenecker, "Acts," in *Expositor's Bible Commentary,* vol. 9, ed. Gaebelein, 481.

2. Longenecker, "Acts," 481.

3. I. Howard Marshall, "Acts," in *Tyndale New Testament Commentaries* (1963; reprint, Grand Rapids: Eerdmans, 1989), 293.

4. Ibid.

5. *Tentmaker* refers more generally to "leather worker" and probably is the better meaning in this context. See ibid.

6. Longenecker, "Acts," 481.

7. Robert E. Picirilli, *Paul the Apostle* (Chicago: Moody Press, 1986), 108–9.

8. W. Harold Mare, "1 Corinthians," in *Expositor's Bible Commentary,* vol. 10, ed. Gaebelein, 176.

9. For more detailed discussion on the background of Ephesus and Paul's fruitful three-year ministry there, see Richard N. Longenecker, *The Ministry and Message of Paul* (Grand Rapids: Zondervan, 1971), 69–75.

10. Marshall, "Acts," 292.

11. Ben Witherington, *Women in the Earliest Churches* (Cambridge: Cambridge University Press, 1988), 153–54.

12. Ibid., 114.

13. Everett F. Harrison, "Romans," in *Expositor's Bible Commentary*, vol. 10, ed. Gaebelein, 163.

14. Aquila was, of course, also gifted in these ways. But for our purposes here, we have spotlighted Priscilla alone.

15. See also McReynolds, "Priscilla."

Chapter 9: *Women in Rome*

1. See A. Boyd Luter, "One Little Corner of the World: Localizing the Great Commission," *Christian Education Today* (Fall 1987) for a discussion of the practical significance of this point in regard to Paul's twin strategy (i.e., wider apostolic ministry and person-by-person outreach of local churches) for carrying out Christ's Great Commission in a popular style. As is also brought out in that article, Paul had not founded the church in Colossae, nor had he been there (Col. 2:1). Still, his influence was quite direct in the Colossian church because it was undoubtedly planted as part of the overflow of the apostle's lengthy ministry in Ephesus, in which the entire Roman province in which both Ephesus and Colossae were located was saturated with the gospel (Acts 19:8–10).

2. For a more detailed discussion, see T. Y. Mullins, "Greeting as a New Testament Form," *Journal of Biblical Literature* 87 (1968): 418–26.

3. Royce G. Gruenler, "Romans," in *Evangelical Commentary on the Bible,* ed. Elwell, 955.

4. There are only twenty additional uses of this term for greetings in the rest of the New Testament combined.

5. Largely as a result of this proportion of female names and related descriptions, Romans 16 has proven to be the most popular passage in feminist rewriting of New Testament history. See, e.g., Elizabeth Schussler Fiorenza, "Missionaries, Apostles, Co-Workers: Romans 16

and the Reconstruction of Women's Early Christian History," *Word and World* 4 (1986): 420–33.

6. Tucker and Liefeld, *Daughters of the Church*, 72, strongly assert that *ten* women are mentioned and (citing Peter Richardson) note that this proportion is "startling." On the question of whether there is a tenth woman named by Paul in Romans 16, see Ray R. Schultz, "Romans 16.7: Junia or Junias?" *Expository Times* 98 (1986–87): 108–10.

7. Everett F. Harrison, "Romans," in *Expositor's Bible Commentary*, vol. 10, ed. Gaebelein, 161.

8. Harrison surmises that Phoebe may well have been a successful businesswoman, like Lydia in Philippi (Acts 16). Ibid.

9. It is not possible to be certain whether the position of deacon started in the resolving of the need of the Jerusalem church in Acts 6:1–5, since only the verb *diakoneo* is found there. However, in keeping with Jesus' emphasis on servant-leadership, the clear focus of that passage is also proper servanthood by both the apostles (6:2, 4) and the other disciples (6:1) in leadership roles (6:3, 5).

10. In Romans 16:1 the question is almost a toss-up, though several other key passages and theological and historical considerations must also be carefully weighed in drawing a balanced final conclusion.

11. Leon Morris, *The Epistle to the Romans*, Pillar Commentaries (Grand Rapids: Eerdmans, 1988), 530. Tucker and Liefeld, *Daughters of the Church*, 72–73, add that *prostatis* carries "a strong connotation of leadership and authority."

12. It is highly doubtful that this woman is either Mary, the mother of Jesus; Mary Magdalene; Mary of Bethany; or either of the other two Marys mentioned in the New Testament.

13. Rienecker, *Linguistic Key*, 384.

14. Gruenler, "Romans," 956; Morris, *Romans*, 533.

15. Morris, *Romans*, 533.

16. The possibility that these two were apostles on par with Paul in authority is much less plausible. It can certainly be argued that some of the apostolic functions extended beyond the narrower band of the apostles in the upper room in Acts 1:15–26, plus Paul (Gal. 1:1, 15–17). Nevertheless, the realization that the apostles were a crucial part of the once-for-all undergirding foundation of the church of Jesus Christ (Eph. 2:20) virtually rules out the view that the position (office) of apostle continued. To their credit, in spite of their feminist leanings,

Tucker and Liefeld, *Daughters of the Church*, 73–74, cautiously stop short of claiming the "office of an apostle" for Junia.

17. There is an obvious similarity between Paul's words here and Jesus' words, "shrewd as serpents, and innocent as doves" (Matt. 10:16).

18. F. F. Bruce, "The Epistle of Paul to the Romans," in *Tyndale New Testament Commentaries* (Grand Rapids: Eerdmans, 1963), 278.

Chapter 10: *Women in Philippi*

1. A chronological short list of such notable studies would include W. Derek Thomas, "The Place of Women in the Church at Philippi," *Expository Times* 83 (1972): 117–20; F. X. Malinowski, "The Brave Women of Philippi," *Biblical Theology Bulletin* 15 (1983): 60–64; and Lilian Portefaix, *Sisters Rejoice: Paul's Letters to the Philippians and Luke-Acts as Received by First Century Women* (Stockholm: Almqvist and Wikgren, 1988). Significant attention is also given in Witherington, *Women in the Earliest Churches*.

2. For a discussion of "partnership in the gospel" as the overall theme of Philippians, see A. Boyd Luter, "Philippians," in *Evangelical Commentary on the Bible*, ed. Elwell. See also Luter and Lee, "Philippians as Chiasmus."

3. It should be noted that brief references were previously made to "God-fearing women of high standing" (Acts 13:50, NIV) who persecuted Paul and Barnabas in Pisidian Antioch, and to Timothy's mother, Eunice (Acts 16:1). However, there is no detailed development of them as characters within the narrative of Acts.

4. This term may mean either "prayer" or "place of prayer." See the helpful discussion of the textual variant in Philippians 16:13 and the implications of the term in F. F. Bruce, "Acts," in *New International Commentary on the New Testament*, rev. ed. (Grand Rapids: Eerdmans, 1988), 310, note 34.

5. Although there were almost certainly other men who came to faith before the jailer, whether from Lydia's household (Acts 16:15), the husbands of other women at prayer with Lydia (Acts 16:13) who were converted, or those who were evangelized in the city (perhaps in the wake of the spiritual release of the slave girl in Acts 16:18), the silence in the biblical text certainly leaves the impression that the Philippian church was initially uniquely female-based.

6. Supporting this reading of the evidence is, e.g., Bruce, "Acts," 7.

7. See Stephen Levinsohn, "Participant Reference in Koine Greek Narrative," in *Linguistics and New Testament Interpretation,* ed. David Alan Black (Nashville: Broadman, 1993), 32.

8. Mention of numerous other women in the greetings section of Romans 16 does not constitute the same level of emphasis as is spoken of here. That does not mean such references are inconsequential, simply less specific or central to the circumstances of that church.

9. An independently researched overall chiastic outlining of Philippians has been published by Charles H. Talbert, "Philippians," in *The Mercer Commentary on the Bible,* ed. Watson E. Mills (Macon: Mercer University Press, 1994). The author would like to express thanks for the gracious interaction of Dr. Talbert.

10. See the development of this outline in Luter and Lee, "Chiasmus," in *New Testament Studies* 41, no. 1 (1995): 89–101.

11. Peter T. O'Brien, "Commentary on Philippians," in *New International Greek Testament Commentary* (Grand Rapids: Eerdmans, 1991), 477–78.

12. Ibid., 478.

13. Ralph P. Martin, *Philippians,* New Century Bible (Grand Rapids: Eerdmans, 1980), 152.

14. Luter and Lee, "Chiasmus," forthcoming.

15. The Greek words are *suzuge, sullambanou, sunethlesan,* and *sunergon* (the underlining indicates the *sun-* prefix). No other verse in Philippians contains more than two *sun-* prefix terms. Interestingly, that verse is 2:25 and the reference is to Epaphroditus, who will soon return to Philippi to help (as a "partner") the church deal with the problems at hand (2:25–30).

16. See also the brief but helpful discussion of Lydia in Tucker and Liefeld, *Daughters of the Church,* 68–69.

17. Admittedly, Acts 16 does not specifically say that the slave-girl was converted, but it is very unlikely that she would have been sandwiched between Lydia and the jailer if she had not also become a believer.

18. For whatever reasons, Tucker and Liefeld, *Daughters of the Church,* 71, limit mention of Euodia and Syntyche to two sentences.

19. Fred Craddock, "Philippians," in *Interpretation* (Atlanta: John Knox, 1985), 70.

20. Martin, *Philippians,* 152.

21. A more scholarly presentation of much of this material is Luter, "Partners in the Gospel."

Chapter 11: *Eunice*

1. It should be realized that when 2 Corinthians 6:14 says, literally, "do not be unequally yoked together with unbelievers" it is stating a principle that has broad application to "those relationships in which the degree of association entails an inevitable compromise with Christian standards of conduct" (James A. Davis, "2 Corinthians," in *Evangelical Commentary on the Bible*, ed. Elwell, 990). Certainly, a Christian marrying a non-Christian is, at best, dangerous in regard to keeping biblical standards, if not doomed in many instances.

2. This appears to be the major reason why Eunice is only mentioned in passing by Tucker and Liefeld, *Daughters of the Church*, 68.

3. A highly readable development of the remarkable relationship between Paul and Timothy is William J. Peterson, *The Discipling of Timothy* (Wheaton: Victor, 1980).

4. A more extensive discussion of this disagreement, primarily focusing on Barnabas and John Mark, is found in Luter, *Looking Back, Moving On*, 83–85.

5. Levinsohn, "Participant Reference," 32–33.

6. William H. Baker, "Acts," in *Evangelical Commentary on the Bible*, ed. Elwell, 912.

7. Some believe that Timothy's father was dead by this point. However, since the only references to him are in Acts 16:1, 3, simply mentioning that he was a Greek, there is not enough information to back that view.

8. Sir William Ramsay, cited by Bruce, "Acts," 304.

9. Eunice's mother, Lois, probably had little to do with the match, and the timing was certainly many years before either Eunice or Lois became believers in Christ (2 Tim. 1:5).

10. See the helpful discussion in Polhill, "Acts," 342–43.

11. This possibility is discussed at some length by S. J. D. Cohen, "Was Timothy Jewish (Acts 16:1–3)?" *Journal of Biblical Literature* 105 (1986): 251–68.

12. See the plausible reconstructions of the sequence and timing of events in Paul's ministry in, e.g., D. A. Carson, Douglas Moo, and Leon Morris, *An Introduction to the New Testament* (Grand Rapids:

Zondervan, 1992), 228–31; and John Piper, "Chronology, New Testament," in *Baker Encyclopedia of the Bible*, gen. ed. Walter A. Elwell (Grand Rapids: Baker, 1988) 1:445–48.

13. Lewis Foster, "Acts," *New International Version Study Bible*, gen. ed. Kenneth Barker (Grand Rapids: Zondervan, 1985), 1676.

14. It is almost certainly not a coincidence that Paul, in later writing to Timothy and clarifying the qualifications for an elder/overseer, uses the same idea, translated "good reputation" (NASB, NIV), in 1 Timothy 3:7.

15. Apparently, Timothy's primary spiritual gift was in the realm of preaching and teaching (1 Tim. 4:13–14). The laying on of hands by the elders spoken of in 1 Timothy 4:14 was most likely either a confirmation of his gifting by the leaders in his home church or some sort of an informal ordination service related to Timothy's fitness for ministry (G. W. Knight III, "1–2 Timothy/Titus," in *Evangelical Commentary on the Bible*, ed. Elwell, 1107).

16. Luke is seen to be a Gentile because he is listed *after* "the only Jews among my fellow workers" (Col. 4:11, 14 NIV). His joining up with Paul in ministry is likely inferred in the change in the author's perspective from "they" to "we" (i.e., as present and participating) in Acts 16:10, only a few months after Timothy was chosen (16:1–3).

17. Just how painful adult circumcision was can be seen from the trick that Jacob's sons used to kill the Shechemites in Genesis 34. On the third day after being circumcised, all the men of Shechem were still in too much pain to defend themselves against attack (34:24–25).

18. The personal letter that Paul wrote to Philemon, a member of the church in Colossae (that can be determined by comparing Col. 4:9 with Philem. 10–17), is strong evidence that additional correspondence beyond formal doctrinal epistles was going on between Paul's missionary band and those with whom they were close. Also, since Timothy's name was included as a sort of cowriter with Paul from the beginning (1 Thess. 1:1), it would seem Timothy certainly had the authority to write.

19. It is, of course, possible that Timothy did get back to Central Asia Minor at some point while Paul was being held in Caesarea (Acts 23:31–26:32). The biblical text is silent on the whereabouts of Timothy during that period.

20. Baker, "Acts," 920, states, "Most evangelicals believe" that the Apostle was released after the lapse of the "statutory limit for Paul's accusers to state their case."

21. By this time Timothy was probably thirty years old or slightly older. In that day, though, "a person between 30 and 40 years old could be considered young," possibly not to the age of "discernment" (Rienecker, *Linguistic Key,* 627).

22. Knight, "1–2 Timothy/Titus," 1099, gives this range of possible dates of 1 Timothy and 2 Timothy, assuming the most common evangelical reconstruction of events in the final years of Paul's life.

Chapter 12: *Women as Disciples*

1. For further study on women disciples, see the following bibliography and the entries on the various women disciples in the New Testament in Paul Gardner, ed., *The Complete Who's Who of the Bible* (Grand Rapids: Zondervan, Spring, 1995). Also, for the wider scope of New Testament discipleship in connection with recovery counseling issues, see A. Boyd Luter and Kathy McReynolds, *Disciplined Living: What the New Testament Says about Discipleship and Recovery* (Grand Rapids: Baker, 1996).

2. There is, however, no absolutely clear-cut evidence that any of these women held office within the structure for New Testament church government laid out in 1 Timothy 3:1–13 and Titus 1:5–9.

3. See the discussion of the Junia controversy in chapter 9.

4. It is our studied conviction that God gave Scriptural truth into time and space that we might draw timeless principles for timely application in our lives. For further development of that perspective, see A. Boyd Luter, "How to Interpret and Apply the Bible," *New American Standard Study Bible,* ed. George Giacumakis (La Habra, Calif.: Lockman Foundation, forthcoming). For a recent source of distilled wisdom in regard to the practical application of the Bible, see Jack Huhatchek, *Taking the Guesswork out of Applying the Bible* (Downers Grove, Ill.: InterVarsity Press, 1990).

5. Such a contagious passion for discipleship is evident throughout Wilkins, *Following the Master,* which the authors highly recommend.

SELECTED BIBLIOGRAPHY

Both the more popular and more in-depth or scholarly resources below were chosen because of their focus (in whole or in part) on women and/or disciples in the New Testament. Most have been written since 1980 and thus are relatively current. It should be noted that there has been something of a scarcity of writing on women disciples in the New Testament, except in feminist (whether evangelical, liberal, or Catholic) circles. This volume will help remedy that unfortunate shortage.

Chapin, Shelly. "Women in the Bible." In *The Complete Who's Who of the Bible*. Ed. Paul Gardner. Grand Rapids: Zondervan, 1995.

Collins, Raymond F. "Mary Magdalene," "Mary of Bethany." In *Anchor Bible Dictionary*. 6 vols. Gen. ed. David Noel Freedman. Garden City, N.Y.: Doubleday, 1992.

D'Angelo, Mary Rose. "Women in Luke-Acts: A Redactional View." *Journal of Biblical Literature* 109 (1990): 441–61.

Gilman, Florence M. "Eunice," "Euodia." In *Anchor Bible Dictionary*. 6 vols. Gen. ed. David Noel Freedman. Garden City, N.Y.: Doubleday, 1992.

Heine, Susanne. *Women and Early Christianity: A Reappraisal*. Minneapolis: Augsburg, 1988.

Hurley, James B. *Man and Woman in Biblical Perspective.* Grand Rapids: Zondervan, 1981.

Luter, A. Boyd. "Great Commission." In *Anchor Bible Dictionary.* 6 vols. Gen. ed. David Noel Freedman. Garden City, N.Y.: Doubleday, 1992.

———. *A New Testament Theology of Discipling.* Ann Arbor: University Microfilms, 1985.

———. "Partners in the Gospel: The Role of Women in the Church at Philippi." *Journal of the Evangelical Theological Society* (1997).

———. "The Prominence of Women in Philippians and the Church at Philippi." Paper presented at the Society of Biblical Literature, Pacific Coast Region, Santa Clara, California, 1994.

———. "Tabitha/Dorcas (Acts 9:36–43): A Model Disciple?" Paper presented at the Evangelical Theological Society, Far West Region, Sun Valley, California, April 1994.

McReynolds, Kathy. "Aquila," "Elizabeth," "Hannah," "Joanna," "Martha," "Mary Magdalene," "Mary, the Mother of Jesus," "Priscilla," "The Samaritan Woman," "Susanna." In *The Complete Who's Who of the Bible.* Ed. Paul Gardner. Grand Rapids: Zondervan, 1995.

Munro, Winsome. "Women Disciples in Mark?" *Catholic Biblical Quarterly* 44 (1982): 225–41.

Osborne, Grant R. "Women in Jesus' Ministry." *Westminster Theological Journal* 51 (1989): 259–91.

Pape, Dorothy. *In Search of God's Ideal Woman.* Downers Grove, Ill.: InterVarsity Press, 1976.

Petersen, William J. *The Discipling of Timothy.* Wheaton: Victor, 1980.

Ryan, Rosalie. "Lydia, A Dealer in Purple Goods." *The Bible Today* 22 (1984): 285–99.

———. "The Women from Galilee and Discipleship in Luke." *Biblical Theology Bulletin* 15 (1985): 56–59.

Scholer, David. "Women." In *Dictionary of Jesus and the Gospels.* Ed. Joel B. Green, Scot McKnight, and I. Howard Marshall. Downers Grove, Ill.: InterVarsity Press, 1992.

Schreiner, Thomas R. "The Valuable Ministries of Women in the Context of Male Leadership." In *Recovering Biblical Manhood and Womanhood.* Ed. John Piper and Wayne Grudem. Wheaton: Crossway, 1991.

Schultz, Ray R. "Romans 16:7: Junia or Junias?" *Expository Times* 98 (1986–87): 108–10.

Schussler-Fiorenza, Elizabeth. *In Memory of Her.* New York: Crossroad, 1983.

———. "Missionaries, Apostles, Coworkers: Romans 16 and the Reconstruction of Women's Early Christian History." *Word and World* 4 (1986): 420–33.

Sigountos, James, and Myron Shank. "Public Roles for Women in the Pauline Church: A Reappraisal of the Evidence." *Journal of the Evangelical Theological Society* 26 (1983): 283–95.

Stagg, Evelyn, and Frank Stagg. *Women in the World of Jesus.* Philadelphia: Westminster Press, 1978.

Tetlow, Elizabeth. *Women and Ministry in the New Testament: Called to Serve.* New York: Paulist Press, 1980.

Thomas, W. Derek. "The Place of Women in the Church at Philippi." *Expository Times* 83 (1971–72): 117–20.

Tucker, Ruth A., and Walter L. Liefeld. *Daughters of the Church: Women and Ministry from New Testament Times to the Present.* Grand Rapids: Academie/Zondervan, 1987.

Wilkins, Michael J. "Disciple," "Discipleship." In *Dictionary of Jesus and the Gospels.* Ed. Joel B. Green, Scot McKnight, and I. Howard Marshall. Downers Grove, Ill.: InterVarsity Press, 1992.

———. *Following the Master: Discipleship in the Footsteps of Jesus.* Grand Rapids: Zondervan, 1992.

———. "Named and Unnamed Disciples in the Gospel of Matthew: A Literary/Theological Study." In *Society of Biblical Literature Seminary Papers* vol. 30. Atlanta: Scholars Press, 1991.

Witherington, Ben. "Dorcas," "Euodia," "Women." In *Anchor Bible Dictionary.* 6 vols. Gen. ed. David Noel Freedman. Garden City, N.Y.: Doubleday, 1992.

———. "On the Road with Mary Magdalene, Joanna, Susanna and Other Disciples: Luke 8:1–3." *Zeitschrift für die Neutestamentliche Wissenschaft* 70 (1979): 243–48.

———. *Women in the Earliest Churches.* Cambridge: Cambridge University Press, 1988.

———. *Women in the Ministry of Jesus.* Cambridge: Cambridge University Press, 1984.

For further information on specific women disciples in the New Testament, consult standard evangelical commentaries as well as other recent Bible dictionaries and encyclopedias. Also, a number of additional related studies are referenced in the notes for the various chapters of this book, and most of those resources note other potentially relevant items.

Boyd Luter (B.S., Mississippi State University; Th.M., Ph.D., Dallas Theological Seminary) is adjunct professor of biblical studies at Golden Gate Baptist Theological Seminary: Southern California Campus. He has written several books on recovery, discipleship, and Bible exposition and contributed to such biblical resource works as the *Evangelical Commentary on the Bible, Anchor Bible Dictionary,* and *The Complete Who's Who of the Bible.*

Kathy McReynolds (B.A., Biola University; M.A., Talbot School of Theology) contributed to the *Life Recovery Bible* and *The Complete Who's Who of the Bible.* She has team-taught a theology of recovery course with Dr. Luter at Talbot School of Theology.